CHANGE YOUR BUSINESS

CHANGE YOUR LIFE

Hudi

Overcoming the Obstacles In Your Path:

A Guide For Small Business Owners

Enjoy!

Michael Stelter

Contents

WHO IS THIS BOOK FOR?

Change is the only constant in life. Nothing stays still; everything is always changing. The only question is, is it changing for better or worse? Are you in control of the change, or are you letting it happen *to* you?

I am a change agent. If you don't want to change, or to have your business change, then you don't want to work with me. But if you want your business to change for the better, to change in the ways that you desire— that's what I help you do.

Every business and every business owner is different, but there are just two things that determine whether you, as a business owner, will be successful at producing the change you want:

1. Desire to grow your business

2. Willingness to change the way you are doing things

With these two things in place, I have never found a problem that we could not fix together.

So to determine if you will be able to make the change you wish to see in your business, ask yourself these questions:

1. Why do you want to grow your business?

2. Are you willing to REALLY change the way you look at your business, your customers, and yourself?

Are you comfortable with both those answers?

Good! Let's move on to...

What makes a business successful?

The answer is surprisingly simple, yet so many people are unaware of it. Every business is a *direct reflection* of its owner.

If the owner is disorganized, the business will be, too. If the owner is selfish, it will reflect in their employees and the way they interact with customers. If the business owner lives in chaos and drama, those things will find their way into their business, and the result is never positive.

Business owners tend to hire people like themselves. Employees also tend to learn how they should think and feel about the business from the owner. If the owner is frustrated with the business and feels it's not worth their time, the employees will feel that way, too.

So many of the changes that need to be made are within the mind, attitude and perception of the owner. That is why you must have a willingness to change what *you* are doing if you wish to change your business.

The good news is, all these things are under our ultimate control! Most of us simply never realize that, or never take the steps necessary to change ourselves to produce the reality we want.

To create the business you want, you must first know what that successful business looks like. You must know exactly how much money you wish to make, how much time you wish to spend at the business, how you wish your employees to behave, etc.

Many business owners never take the time to create that vision and write out this detailed business plan, which is why their business ends up looking quite different from what they subconsciously expected!

Ask one hundred business owners to define 'SUCCESS,' and you will get at least one hundred different answers. Some definitions include...

- Improved quality of life

- More time with family and friends

- A strong work/life balance

- Delivering a quality product

- Enough money to do what they want, when they want

- A flexible schedule

- The ability to be away from work and still make money

What is *your* definition of a successful business?

While on their entrepreneurial path, every small business owner is likely to face these same four obstacles that must be overcome to enjoy their version of success:

MONEY

Money is often seen as the prime benefit of owning your own business, but that is not always so. Here are a few of the most common money issues experienced by business owners:

- There is never enough money in the checking account at the end of the month.

- The rules of marketing and advertising are constantly changing. We don't seem to be getting a return on our investment.

- I have opportunities to grow the business, but need money to invest to make that happen, and can't/don't want to get it from the bank.

- By the time I pay all the bills and my employees, there is nothing left for me.

- Although we're busier than we've ever been, profit has not gone up.

Do any of these issues sound familiar to you? Read on, and through the parable of Mary and the Missing Money — a business owner and single mom with a special needs daughter — we'll learn how you can grow your business without giving away your life.

TIME

Each day, every person is given the same amount of time. Sixty seconds in a minute, sixty minutes in each hour, twenty-four hours each day, seven days a week, 365 days each year. It's what we do with our time that matters.

A common problem with time is that the amount of time being invested in the business has taken away any work/life balance the owner may have once had. Here are a few common time issues experienced by small business owners:

- Working 60+ hours a week

- Saying things like "My customers come to my business because of me and what I do" or "If I wasn't here, my customers would go somewhere else."

- Having family relationship troubles with spouse and/or children

- Suffering from health issues that constantly resurface, such as lack of sleep, anxiety, headaches, etc.

In the parable of Mark and the Disappearing Time, we will address the common mistakes business owners make that can leave their businesses crippled when they're not around — and leave the owner imprisoned by responsibility!

TEAM

As a business grows, the only way to scale and grow consistently is to add employees. But just because you are a good (add any product/service provider here) doesn't make you a good leader. When a business owner has not developed their inner leader, this is what happens:

- No matter who they hire, no one seems willing to follow directions.

- After a few weeks, the person interviewed seems to be different than the person hired.

- When the owner is not there, nothing ever gets done.

- No one has the same work ethic as the owner.

- The owner struggles to find sales and marketing people that can open doors and build relationships with prospective clients.

In the parable of Joan and the Troubled Team, we'll see how business owners can ensure they are taking optimum advantage of their employees' strengths, and motivating employees to be invested in the business.

EXIT

This problem is most common for business owners in their fifties and older that have been working in the business for years and feel burnt out.

They see the golden gates of retirement beckoning them forward but have just realized that their biggest asset is their business, and they may feel as though selling their business for retirement cash is daunting or impossible.

You will hear them say things like...

- How much is my business worth?

- Who would be interested in buying my business? How do I find them?

- I'd like to retire, but who will run the business if I'm not here?

- How do I convert the business I've built into cash for my retirement?

- Making sure that we have written systems for all important internal processes will increase the value of my company and my retirement cash... now I just need to figure out how to do that.

In the parable of Jack and the Elusive Retirement, we'll see the path of a long-time business owner that finds his way from business ownership to retirement.

#

If you find yourself recognizing some of these problems and nodding in agreement with the lists, then this is the book for you!

Whether you're just starting out or have been at it for decades, there *are* proven principles, practices, tools and techniques that can help you achieve success in all areas of your business.

In my twenty-seven years helping business owners, I have personally witnessed these strategies succeed time after time.

If you have the desire to grow and the willingness to change, you will be successful. The outcome is virtually assured — the only unknown is how long it will take.

Everyone's driving force is different, but the one thing that is always a prerequisite to success is the courage to discover your true motivations.

If you are ready to rethink your perceptions and find out what you really want, please join me and see what **Change Your Business, Change Your Life** can do for you!

MARY AND THE MISSING MONEY

CHAPTER 1

It started with a click. Ever since she was six, Mary loved taking pictures. Pictures of her puppy, of her little brother's laughing face, pictures of the yellow flowers poking their heads up from the garden. No matter what it was, she found a way to capture it.

Mary's love for photography never left her. In fact, the one time she wasn't behind the camera was the day she married Ben, a strapping young fireman whom she had fallen madly in love with.

At first, Ben spent his days at the fire station while Mary spent her days working as a cashier in a retail store.

"Who needs money when we have love?" Mary often thought blissfully to herself. When they did need extra cash, Mary did small, part-time photography projects on the side.

The days swept by in a whirl of joy until the birth of their first child, Eva.

Eva was born with Down's Syndrome. Mary and Ben loved Eva with all their hearts but having just love wasn't enough. They needed more money — and lots of it — so that they could provide the expensive therapy and healthcare Eva needed.

Holding her newborn in exhaustion after giving birth, Mary had a premonition.

In front of her eyes, she saw years flying by in a blur. Soon her small, precious bundle would be old enough for school. Their family would need the money to pay for a school where Eva would get the extra attention she required. Mary and Ben's combined salaries plus the money from her part-time photography work were no longer enough.

The healthcare expenses to give Eva what she needed were likely to continue for the rest of their lives. And as Eva grew, Mary realized that Eva would need specialized care and supervision. Mary was not comfortable leaving her with a low-cost babysitter, or with the thought of leaving her home alone even as a teenager.

With Ben at the firehouse and Mary working a nine-to-five job, who would be there for Eva? Something had to change.

Mary began to look inside herself. What was she good at? What was she able to do that others could not? In a flash, it came to her. Photography.

Mary quit her retail job and devoted her full attention to her photography business. Her goal was to have a flexible schedule and make enough money to provide for Eva's needs with photography as her sole source of income.

Over the next four years, Mary's photography business grew. At first, she was ecstatic. The money was finally coming in.

But as time went by, her dream started to crumble around her. She was working at the business full-time and had grown the business to generate a six-figure revenue over the past four years. But as revenue went up, the time she had to spend with Ben and Eva went down.

Working from home was supposed to be a golden paradise — she would have time to relax, perhaps blissfully collapse into her favorite armchair after a thank you call from an ecstatic client.

Instead, Mary found herself fielding one crisis after another as she struggled to manage her business. Juggling her laundry in one hand and cell phone in the other, it seemed impossible to focus on making more money while keeping her home life intact.

Her schedule was erratic: A typical afternoon was straight from a photo shoot to pick up Eva from school, then head back to the studio to do edits for last week's wedding. She often struggled to find enough time to spend with Eva at home, and that made her routine business tasks take even longer.

Sometimes, it seemed like she had to re-do the bulk of her work because of these frequent starts and stops. And Mary hated that caring for her daughter herself now felt like an afterthought, in the midst of making enough money to pay her medical bills.

Profit from her business covered medical expenses for the family, including a now six-year-old Eva. But something had been lost.

"We never have time to just talk anymore," Mary confided in Ben one spring morning before he left for work.

Then the other shoe dropped. Ben had been complaining about Mary's lack of attention to him for far too long. One bleak morning, those fateful words left his mouth, "I want a divorce."

Mary was devastated. How could Ben leave her, and his daughter? She knew he wasn't equipped to take care of Eva by himself—he would have had to give up his job at the fire station, and he didn't have another plan for making money. He was willing to share expenses but needed a change.

They separated a month later, and the divorce was completed shortly afterwards. Without two pairs of hands on deck, Mary's workload doubled.

Beyond frazzled, Mary confessed to her mother—and proposed an idea.

Eva's grandmother had lived alone since her husband had passed last year. Mary asked if her mother would be interested in moving in with Mary and Eva. She would have time to reconnect with her daughter and granddaughter, and could care for Eva when Mary was wrapped up in business. Fortunately, Mary's mom liked the idea and was happy to help.

Mary had an idea to increase income. If expenses were rising because of her increasing sales, more revenue would solve the problem... wouldn't it? More sales must be the answer.

With new resolve, Mary left her home that morning with a stack full of business cards which she handed out to everyone she passed: the florist, the butcher, the dog walker with chihuahuas in tow.

Over the next few months, her networking began to pay off. More people knew about her business. They wanted to hire her. A local restaurant hired her to take menu pictures.

She was getting more weddings. The florist asked her to shoot flowers for an ad they were creating. She even landed the yearbook photo shoot at the local high school. A real estate company hired her to take pictures of their listed houses.

This new stream of business seemed promising. Unfortunately, many of her new projects came with unexpected drawbacks.

For instance, the real estate photography was time-consuming. To add insult to injury, the company gave her short notice and they took too long to pay. The hours were irregular and impossible to depend on. They wanted her to be available all the time, but rarely called her for work.

Mary felt trapped. How was she supposed to grow her business when customers were so undependable?

She started thinking about why she began doing photography. Yes, she needed the money for Eva's therapy and care, but it was more than that.

"I love it. I always did," Mary said to the plant on the kitchen counter. "There's nothing like getting the perfect shot after hours of trying to get it exactly right. I could have started any business. But I chose photography because that's what I love to do. *So why don't I feel like I love it anymore?*"

The plant remained motionless. Walking away, Mary sighed to herself. Somewhere along the way, her passion had turned into a chore.

When she started her business, Mary knew that running it would entail learning new things and getting out of her comfort zone. But she had no idea that so much of keeping her business going had nothing to do with photography...

For one thing, there never seemed to be enough money in the bank. Not only that, her income was inconsistent, which stretched her nerves as tight as a hot telephone wire.

Some months were great, but on other months, income was little to nothing. In those months, she would ramp up her marketing, only to find herself swamped with too many projects in the next month.

The first few years in business, she saw lots of growth. But now, growth had slowed to a trickle. At the same time, costs for equipment and transportation kept going up.

Because costs were rising, Mary hesitated to dump her more troublesome customers. Could she really afford to say 'no' to a job? Could she really think about raising her prices, when customers would surely want photographers with the lowest rates?

To compound matters, some customers were slow to pay, and invoicing and sending statements was eating up precious time.

What was supposed to be her perfect world now seemed out of control. Between her phone's constant ringing and the 'ding!' coming from her inbox, Mary was ready to try any method that would solve her problems and put money in the bank.

CHAPTER 2

After Ben left and filed for divorce, Mary's life fell to pieces. She looked down at her hands at odd moments, half-expecting to see them sinking into the desk she clutched. It seemed strange that she should remain static and solid while everything around her changed.

The love of her life had left her, and now she couldn't enjoy her daughter and pay her medical bills at the same time. She felt completely and utterly hopeless.

At times like this, she just needed to go for a walk around the block. Feeling the late afternoon sun on her face and breathing the crisp, fresh fall air soothed some of the pain Mary was feeling.

"What do you want?" whispered a voice from the shadows at the edge of the sidewalk.

Shaking her head angrily, Mary gathered her coat around her and made as if to continue down the street, muttering to herself, "First a divorce. Next I'm hearing voices."

But then, something caught her eye. A business card lay on the sidewalk in front of her, as though it had been carefully placed. It had only three words neatly printed on the paper:

The Change Agent

The voice sounded again, now the voice of a refined, but commanding, man.

"What is it you really want?" he asked.

Startled and slightly fearful, Mary turned around slowly. There was a slender, well-dressed man behind her.

He unbuttoned the jacket of his finely tailored suit in one brief movement and reached into his breast pocket, withdrawing a pen.

"How… How did you do that?" Mary stuttered.

"Excuse me?" inquired the man.

"Appear like that. As if by magic. There was no one behind me a second ago, and I didn't see..." She looked around, trying to figure out where he had come from.

"If one understands a thing, one can do it," the well-dressed stranger replied in a matter-of-fact tone. "Understanding is everything. Do you understand yourself? Your business? More importantly… Do you understand your *why?*"

"How did you know I have a business?" Mary asked, narrowing her eyes.

"No matter," the stranger replied decisively. "If you want to figure out what you want—what you really want—then I can help you. If you are unwilling to question your own perceptions and make changes to the way you do things, then no one can help you, I'm afraid."

With a piercing look, he continued. "Do you know what you *really* want?"

Mary looked at the Change Agent and started to walk away. "Why is that any of your business?"

"Perhaps an introduction is in order," said the man in the dark suit, falling into step beside Mary. "I am known as the Change Agent. I came to understand that your business is in chaos. It may not seem like it from the outside—after all, you're generating sales and you have a pool of customers—but you feel like your life is out of control.

"I am here not to tell you what to do, but to show you that the answers to your problems—even the most devastating!—are already inside of you. I'm here to help," he concluded simply.

"Why?"

The Change Agent shrugged. "It's what I do."

Without knowing why, Mary trusted him.

"My experience in working with small businesses," the Change Agent explained, "is vast. With your permission, I would like to ask you two questions. The only questions that really matter."

Mary nodded her head in approval.

"Do you have a desire to grow your business? And are you willing to change the way you do things?"

Mary heard the words and, as directed, thought carefully about the answers. How did she really feel?

The answer came, from both her heart and mind. "My answer is 'yes' to both questions."

The Change Agent smiled. "Like most things in life and business, one answer leads to more questions... would you like my help?"

Mary hesitated. "Yes, if you're willing to give it."

"Mary," the Change Agent asked amicably, "why did you start this business?"

"To do something I love, and make money while doing it."

"But you are doing both of those things," replied the Change Agent. "So why are you unhappy?"

In a softer voice, Mary said, "When I started, I wanted a way to care for my daughter. A nine-to-five job would have kept me away from my home, and my husband, and..."

Blinking away tears, she forged on determinedly. "Working retail and then coming home to make dinner, I was exhausted. Although starting my photography business helped with some of that, things have changed now. Now that I'm the primary breadwinner for me and Eva, it seems that I'm always putting out one fire after another to keep the money flowing."

Looking at the Change Agent, she saw him nodding encouragingly. Spurred on, she continued, "And the upkeep! So many small tasks, but they all add up to spending less time actually earning money! And now I need to generate more profit to support my family. Sometimes I wonder if I am spending more time working now than when I was working retail!"

The Change Agent's eyes turned kind, peering into hers. "What is it that you really want *now*?"

In one final, frustrated impulse, Mary burst out, "To spend time with Eva and still be able to pay the bills! And, sometimes," she continued sheepishly, "to do what I want, for a change."

The man in the suit nodded. "The first step to understanding is forming a clear picture of *what it is you want*." He placed a special emphasis on the last words. "How do you want your life to change? What will your business look like? And in three years, assuming all these challenges have been overcome, what do you want your life to be like?"

Mary opened her mouth, and then closed it with a soft snap as she realized that the stranger's questions had stumped her.

Like most entrepreneurs, she thought she knew why she was in business. Being asked about her underlying motives led her to realize that she wasn't sure what her utopia really looked like.

Thinking about the future, the puzzle pieces began to assemble in her mind.

"I need to generate more sales. But, I have to do more things that people don't pay for, like marketing, sales and bookkeeping. It's the time I spend on these things that makes it seem impossible."

She spoke in a slightly petulant tone at first, remembering, but a new light of excitement shone in her eyes. "I would like to be able to build my business and care for Eva before and after she goes to school, instead of this constant tug of war between appointments. And I would like to have time, every week, for myself. For a trip to the spa or the movies."

"Good," said the Change Agent. "Two of my questions you have answered fully. You know what needs to change: You need more sales and to reduce the amount of time you spend working on non-billable tasks.

"You also know what you want your life to look like: having a successful and profitable business and the time and money to care for Eva and yourself."

Beetling his brows, he met Mary's eyes again. "But what do you want your business to look like *while you are working?*"

A thousand responses flitted through Mary's mind. Yet again, a simple answer was the one that escaped her lips. "I want running my business to be easy. No, not easy," she hastened to correct herself. "Nothing worthwhile is ever easy. I want it to be *doable*. I want to understand the steps I need to take to get my business where I want it to be."

The Change Agent nodded slowly. "Yes. Understanding is the key. When we next meet, *you* will tell *me* what it is that you don't understand. Remember, the answers are already inside."

With a slight wave of his hand, he was gone!

She was alone on the street once more, confused — but hopeful.

CHAPTER 3

In the coming weeks, Mary couldn't get her conversation with the Change Agent out of her head. His questions nagged her. After over five years as a business owner, Mary was vaguely offended that anyone could ask questions that she didn't know how to answer!

"But I don't know what answers I'm looking for," Mary thought to herself plaintively as she heaved her photography bag onto the kitchen countertop. She'd just returned from a photo shoot of two six-month-old twins who, in her humble opinion, would fail to hold still under general anesthetic.

As she dialed the number of a cold lead her first cousin twice removed had sent her weeks ago, the Change Agent's questions echoed in her mind.

"*What is it that you really want?*" Mary put the phone down with a clatter. If she didn't know the answer to that, how could she ever get it? She'd just keep running the same rat race forever.

It was time, she bravely resolved, to answer those questions once and for all.

Digging up a paper and pen, she thought back to their conversation. Soon, the questions were neatly laid out in front of her:

1. How do you want your life to change?

2. What will your business look like?

3. In thirty-six months, what do you want your life to be like?

Mary held the paper close to her face, then she thrust it out to arm's length. Close or far, these three questions were surprisingly challenging. At every point, she found herself running up against one word: *impossible*. She was so limited by what she believed to be possible that she couldn't even answer what she really wanted. It was difficult, because her mind kept going to *how* she would get it done.

Mary tried thinking about what she would want in a magical world where *anything* was possible.

Over the next hour, she wrote down what would become her vision for the next few years. After many scratch-outs and modifications, it boiled down to a few concrete ideas:

Business Goals

- Increase sales.

- Reduce work hours.

- Hire someone to help with the business tasks.

- Add an intern to help with large projects.

- Increase prices.

Personal Goals

- Make an additional $20,000 per year.

- Work 40 hours instead of 60 hours each week.

- Enjoy the customers I work with.

With Eva in school and no customers booked today, Mary went out to the park to clear her mind. No sooner had she settled on a bench beside a soothing river than she looked up to see a familiar figure striding toward her.

The Change Agent hailed her. "Hello, Mary. Have you thought about our last conversation?"

"Thought about it? I couldn't get it out of my head! I was just working on my goals, like we discussed."

"Fabulous!" he exclaimed. "Of course, there are goals and then there are SMART goals. Not all goals are equal."

"Why? What makes one goal better than another?"

"You see, SMART is an acronym. It stands for…

Specific

Measurable

Achievable

Results-focused

Time-bound.

"If you can form a SMART goal, you will find it easier to track your progress towards achieving it. When you focus your attention and energy on the things that will help you accomplish those SMART goals, there is almost no way you will not reach them," the Change Agent explained.

That sounded pretty good to Mary.

"The best way to form your plan," the Change Agent continued, "is to work backwards. Figure out what your ideal vision is, then work backwards to make a 12-month plan to achieve it. Once you know that, the essential part is to get the ball rolling. For this, you need a 90-day plan.

"So, during the next ninety days, focus on what needs to be stopped, started, or changed to get you to your 12-month plan and 36-month plan."

"It sounds easy enough," Mary agreed reluctantly. She was sure that it couldn't be as easy as the Change Agent said.

The Change Agent laughed. "As you noted when we last met, nothing worthwhile is ever easy — but it is doable! I have faith in you. But you need to figure out what your long-term vision is before you can set your 12-month plan and your 90-day goals."

"Well," said Mary, pleased to report her progress, "I wrote down a list of what I want my life and business to be like in thirty-six months."

"Tremendous!" the man in the suit exclaimed, clapping his hands and taking a seat on the bench beside her. "Now, it is time to figure out what you need to do in the next twelve months to achieve this vision."

Mary looked at him inquiringly, but he shook his head.

"I can't do that for you. I am only here to assist. The answers and the wisdom are all inside. You just need to locate them."

"Well," Mary mused aloud, "I'm going to need to make more cash to cover rising costs. They are taking a huge chunk out of my checkbook. But, if I had money to invest into marketing and sales, I think it would pay off in the long run."

"Continue," the Change Agent nodded encouragingly.

"If I could delegate some tasks or have less of them, I would have more time for Eva, and myself. Maybe I can use that time to get more organized. You see, in elementary school, my desk was always a mess. My backpack was always filled to the brim. My strength is creative, not organizational," Mary finished ruefully.

"Great organizers are sometimes born, this is true," the Change Agent acquiesced with a gentle smile. "*But they are also made.* When you improve yourself as a person—when you learn skills such as organization and time management—you will see your business beginning to improve as if by magic."

"Are you saying that my 12-month plan should also have to do with self-improvement, not just with my business?"

"Ah, but self-development *is* part of your business. Your business is a direct reflection of who you are. This is both a blessing and a curse—it will reflect your best, but also your worst traits," he said.

"I think I see…" Mary mused aloud. "If I become a better business owner over the next year, my business will improve as a result."

"Yes. And I encourage you to never stop learning," the Change Agent replied.

Mary sat for a moment, deep in thought at this idea.

When she looked back, the Change Agent was nowhere to be found!

Remembering what her new friend had said about creating a 12-month plan and setting 90-day SMART goals, she decided to do so on the spot. To the tune of birds chirping near the park bench, she started to write.

12-Month Plan

- Identify at least three ways to increase revenue from current customers.

- Increase hourly rate within the next 12 months to raise yearly revenue.

- Identify the business tasks that need to be done for the health of the business.

  o Determine the amount of time currently spent doing these tasks.

  o Find help to take on those projects.

- Delegate tasks and minimize time-wasting activities to work less each week.

- Find more customers who are easy to work with.

90-Day SMART Goals

1. Within 30 days, determine the profitability and time investment for each type of work.

2. Identify a minimum hourly rate desired and use that as a baseline for future pricing. What is my time worth?

3. Start qualifying new customers by writing up a few questions to ask when we first meet.

4. Start spreading the word to customers, vendors, and other business owners that I am looking for part-time help and a photography intern to teach and mentor.

5. Within 60 days, stop wasting time. Find at least 5 hours/week.

6. Change prices for new prospects by +20%.

7. Within ninety days, change the way sales are generated.

Soon, Mary's resolve was tested. A local summer camp offered her a contract for the summer. Though they were willing to pay well, their communication was patchy, which she knew could create future problems.

The last thing she wanted was to waste time constantly going back and forth over email just to schedule a shoot. And though she loved kids, the idea of being a photographer in a hectic summer camp environment just didn't appeal to her.

The long days away from her work, and Eva, made this a nice job for someone else out there — but it didn't fit Mary's goals.

After penning a polite email to decline the offer and suggesting another photographer that could do the work, it suddenly occurred to Mary that she *had* already changed.

Months ago, she never would have refused a paying customer just because of one or two small things that didn't make the job a good fit for her. Smiling to herself, she remembered the Change Agent's advice about becoming a better business owner.

She was officially on her way.

CHAPTER 4

The sky was getting dark when Mary returned home from a late-afternoon wedding shoot. Grateful to have her mother helping out, but missing Ben desperately, Mary shed a few bittersweet tears in her room. Even though her business was improving, she knew she had a long way to go. Mary felt the familiar knot in her stomach keeping her awake. Attempting the old trick, she tried counting sheep.

After what felt like hours, she found herself in a dream without realizing she had even fallen asleep.

Mary was in a green, hilly pasture, with deep blue skies above. A familiar besuited figure strolled along the grass near her.

"Hello, Mary," said the Change Agent as he sat down on a patch of soft moss. "Isn't it a beautiful day?"

Mary concurred. In the pleasant heat of the sun, she felt more mellow and relaxed than she had in her waking life in some time.

"Let's hear an update on your 90-day goals," said the Change Agent.

"Since we've met," she began, "I've created a solid, long-term vision for my life and my business, and I've identified the things I need to do in the next year to achieve that vision. Then my plan is, every ninety days, to create a list of SMART goals to move me toward my one-year goal."

"Superlative work, Mary!" The Change Agent was clearly pleased. "Today, let us talk about numbers."

"Ugh, numbers," Mary groaned. "They're the bane of my existence," she explained with some drama. "Too many of them, and my head starts to spin."

The Change Agent nodded, commiserating with Mary's plight. "Working with business numbers can be tough. Few people find it to be the most fun part of their day. But numbers are so very useful! They can be powerful allies, if you take the time to befriend them.

"For example, take these Five Key Performance Indicators (KPIs) that allow you to reach your goals. If you don't learn how to use these, reaching them will be much harder! Tracking these numbers weekly is vital so that you can see where you are making the most money — and where you are losing it. You can then adjust what you do according to these findings.

"The 5 KPIs are as follows:

Number of leads

Conversion rate percent

Average dollar amount per sale

Number of transactions per time period

Margin percentage.

"Let us walk through each of them one at a time, beginning with number of leads. Mary, if you were to improve your business, what would you need?"

"More customers, I suppose?" Mary responded quizzically.

"And what's the first step to getting customers?"

"Having leads—people to offer my business to."

"Correct! And I can help you find ways to get more quality leads. I can also show you how to convert more of those leads into real sales. As a result, you will have more customers."

The Change Agent pulled an elegant pen and small leather notebook from his coat pocket and wrote on the top of the first page...

Leads

x Conversion %

= # Customers

"Now, what else do you need in your business?" the Change Agent asked.

"More sales," Mary responded. "But I guess if I had that, I'd have everything I need," she laughed.

The Change Agent smiled. "How do you get more sales?"

"By getting more customers — and more purchases per customer. I'd love it if each of my customers ordered one or two photo shoots per year!" Mary clapped her hands together at the thought.

"Exactly! I can show you," the Change Agent explained, "ways to increase the number of transactions per customer and focus on sales that get you the best dollar amount for your labor.

"Number of transactions is the number of times a customer buys something from you over a period of time. Then, the average dollar per sale is the average amount your customers spend with you on each transaction."

Reaching for the pen and notebook, the Change Agent added to the words on the page...

Leads

x Conversions

= # Customers

x # of Transactions

x Average $ Sale

= Revenue $

"But," he explained, "revenue is just a number. What do you really want to see from the business?" the Change Agent asked.

"More profit," Mary said decisively. "I want to increase my net profit."

"Precisely!" the Change Agent agreed. "That final number we need to talk about is Margin percent — that's the portion of the Revenue that you take home after you pay all your expenses. When you multiply Margin percent times your revenue, the result is your net profit. There are many ways to increase that number as well!"

Again, reaching for the pen and notebook, the Change Agent added to the words on the page...

Leads

x Conversion %

= Customers

x # of Transactions

x Average $ Sale

= Revenue $

x Margin %

= Net Profit

"It is important to understand how these five KPIs work together to impact your business. Now, I'd like you to do two things.

"The first thing is to look back over your records and do your best to identify what each of these numbers was for your business for the last year. It's alright to guess if you don't know a number for sure."

He continued, "Put the five numbers into the formula. When you do the math, you will get the results you are more familiar with in your business... Number of Customers, Total Revenue and Net Profit.

"The second step is to increase each of the KPIs by 10%, then write those new KPI numbers on a separate sheet of paper using the same formulas. After that, recalculate for the Result Numbers. I expect that you may be surprised at the result. When we meet next, you can tell me what you've found!"

The Change Agent's soothing voice was fading as Mary felt herself slipping through the borderlands of sleep. She gave one last glance at the sunny valley before she opened her eyes to find herself, warm and content, in her own bed.

Inexplicably, she found a piece of paper crumpled in her hands.

She smoothed it out to find herself clutching a paper in the Change Agent's handwriting—his formula for her success.

CHAPTER 5

Mary was grateful that her mother had been able to move in with them. It allowed Mary to spend more time with her mother after Dad passed last year, and it gave Mom more time with Eva. Having Mom available to help with Eva even allowed for some special 'me' time away.

It was a breezy spring afternoon when Mary decided to grab a bite at a local Mexican restaurant.

"Table for two?" the waiter asked, looking around for other members of her party.

"No. Just one..." Mary trailed off as she realized that the waiter was walking away, not seeming to have heard her.

He had placed two menus onto the table as she sat down, then hurried off before she could correct his mistake. She imagined Ben sitting across from her, how things had been when they were younger — but she'd learned that that was something she couldn't think about on her special days out to relax.

Mary turned her attention to perusing the menu. She was debating between a grilled tortilla with roasted vegetables and a shrimp salad when someone sat down at her table. She looked up, a little bit alarmed, but was pleased to see the well-dressed man across the table.

The Change Agent was earnestly studying the menu. "Have you ever tried the burritos here? I might try them, but I fear upsetting what is sometimes a delicate stomach."

"I've never had any trouble with them," responded Mary. "I didn't know you would be joining me," she added, smiling despite herself. He was the *only* man she'd like to be sitting across from right now.

"So often the important things that come into our lives are also the things that we least expect. For instance, many business owners never dream that understanding money and cash flow would be the source of not a few of their sleepless nights," the Change Agent said, sampling the free tortilla chips from a basket on their table.

"Delicious!" he pronounced. "Now, where was I? Ah. When we last met, you had some homework to do with your KPIs. What did you learn?"

Looking slightly concerned, Mary shared, "I must have done something wrong. The number I came up with can't possibly be right."

The Change Agent smiled broadly. "Why is that?"

"Well," said Mary, "I had to estimate the numbers for most of my five KPIs because I hadn't been tracking them, so I just guessed so I could get my homework done.

"Then, I increased each of them by 10%. But when I recalculated the results after each number was increased by 10%, the resulting profit was so huge that I'm sure I messed up somewhere!"

"What did the new numbers show you?" inquired the Change Agent.

"My new numbers showed a 21% increase in Customers, a 46% increase in Revenue, and a 61% increase in Net Profit! I must be really bad at math."

"On the contrary, Mary, you're perfectly correct," exclaimed the Change Agent. "That's the magic of those five KPIs for your business. By increasing each one by only 10%, that's exactly the kind of result you can expect.

"There are dozens of strategies to increase each of those numbers by 10%. Not all will work for your business, but many will. In fact, many business owners see increases of more than 10% once they start strategically improving those numbers. Results reaching over 100% for some businesses is not uncommon!"

"Wow!" Mary was shocked. "So, I didn't do the math wrong? And... this really is possible for me? My business can really grow like that, just by working to increase these numbers?"

The Change Agent nodded.

"That's amazing!" Mary exclaimed. "Okay — how do we do that?" she asked eagerly.

The Change Agent tucked his napkin into his collar, anticipating his meal. "Before we take on that long-term project, we need a clear understanding of what additional money could be used for — and how much of it you might need to make these plans happen."

Mary nodded. "I could use investment money to buy new equipment, and cash to cover the costs for some help to get the work done. I already spread the word that I'm looking for an intern. Sometimes I think that if I was able to hire an assistant, I would be able to take on larger and more lucrative jobs."

"Yes," the Change Agent concurred. "Many businesses struggle to find the money they need to support growth. They wonder why it's so difficult. In business, you have four options to access cash to fuel growth:

1. Increase revenue

2. Reduce expenses

3. Borrow it from a lender

4. Get an investor

"Options three and four allow you to get cash *before* you grow, but they also come with their own costs. Both will require you to share your financial information with outsiders and prove that your business is profitable enough to provide your lender or investor with good returns.

"Lenders, of course, also charge interest on money lent; and investors will receive a portion of the profits you obtain through your growth and may want to have some say in how your company is run.

"Whether you plan to grow without outside help or look for lenders or investors, you will need to be organized and have a good understanding of your business's cash flow potential.

"For this and other reasons we'll discuss, you need an organized financial plan and reports. This step will make you a better business owner because you will understand your business's financials on a much deeper level than just watching the money flow in and out of your checkbook. And then, if you choose, these reports will help you get the capital you need.

"Today, we will find out what you need to do to create an organized financial plan.

"But first, an important question... What is money?" queried the Change Agent.

Mary blinked at this turn of conversation. "Well... it's a form of exchange, I suppose. We use it to trade with one another."

"In one way, you are right," the Change Agent agreed. "It is a form of exchange. But the missing piece to your answer is vital. What are we exchanging? So crucial, yet so simple.

"The intangible, unutterably valuable thing we use money to exchange for is—energy." The Change Agent finished his proclamation with an air of a grand pronouncement.

Slightly underwhelmed, Mary asked, "You mean, the energy we use to work?"

"I mean that money *is* energy," the Change Agent repeated with a smile. "It can make things happen. Those who understand money can use it to make our dreams and desires a reality!

"This is particularly important to a business. A small business owner often sees money as the measure of their success.

"First, they strive to generate money in the form of sales. Then they spend some of that money on inventory, supplies and labor. Eventually, they use business financials as a 'report card' of their ability to run the business."

Mary nodded. That sounded familiar to her!

"But the truth is that money is energy," the Change Agent repeated. "If the energy you put into the business exceeds the amount of energy the business provides to you in the form of profit—then your business is not successful, no matter what its report card says!"

Their meals arrived, and the Change Agent dug into his burrito with gusto.

"The financial plan should be to balance your sales, your variable expenses, your fixed expenses, and your planned net profit. The key is to do this without compromising your people, customers, suppliers, processes, or levels of quality.

"Sounds like a tall order, right? The way we do this is with your business financial reports." The Change Agent took a huge bite of his burrito.

Mary agreed. "I am sometimes tempted to take on more customers to increase sales, but that often increases my expenses and eats my time. Then that compromises my quality because I can't maintain the same level of focus on my work."

"Exactly," said the Change Agent. "It's a balancing act. What you need to do is create systems that support this goal of a balanced business. For example, one of your challenges is customers who pay late. What could you do to minimize this risk?"

"I could ask customers to give a 50% deposit before the project starts. That way, I would be assured of at least half of the payment beforehand, which would be a huge help for cash flow." Gaining confidence, Mary continued, "That would discourage slow payers from hiring me, and I'd have more time for customers who pay promptly!"

"Good!" The Change Agent punctuated this statement by gesturing with the burrito he held precariously in his hand. With his suit jacket draped over his chair, he looked surprisingly youthful.

"But we have drifted slightly off topic. The question is, how can you gain control of the money coming into, and going out of, your business? Whatever you create needs to track sales, all your expenses and your take-home profit."

Thinking for a moment, Mary sipped her drink. "I know there is software that can track all those things, because I bought it. But I never learned to use it. This might sound silly, but if there is money in the checking account at the end of the month, it's been a good month."

"I see," said the Change Agent, now moving on to his salad. "It's important to track your numbers for two reasons: One, these financial reports are your business owner report card — they will tell you how you're doing. The second is that you can't improve something if it can't be measured. If your measure of success is 'there is money left,' you are unlikely to ever end up with *more* money left. You see?"

"That makes sense," Mary said. "I'll get to work on this right away."

"Splendid." The Change Agent finished his meal, dusted off his hands with his napkin and stood to leave. "Until next time," he said. "Thank you for a delicious meal and splendid conversation."

Mary finished her meal in thoughtful silence. When she asked for the bill, she found it had already been paid.

CHAPTER 6

One of Mary's SMART goals was to start asking qualifying questions of new prospects. Asking a few simple questions on the phone saved time for her and her prospect, and she could increase the chances she would find another good customer she wanted to work with.

Instead of repeating her past mistakes, she was determined to learn. On her morning trip to the grocery store, she jotted down a list of common problems with her not-so-good customers on the side of her shopping list. It came out like this:

- ~~milk~~ Slow payers

- ~~butter~~ Short notice for projects

- ~~jalapeno peppers~~ Irregular hours

- ~~bread~~ Unreasonable demands

- ~~laundry soap~~ Poor communication

Looking at this dog-eared list, Mary could see that she, in the past, had ignored these issues because she wanted to make more sales. Yet the projects she had taken with troublesome customers only served to sap her energy and take time away from the other work she really enjoyed.

Mary was about to exit the grocery when her shopping cart careened into another one with a loud crash!

"Oh, I'm so sorry," she exclaimed, bending down to pick up a package of Jell-O that had tumbled to the floor.

"No need to worry," a familiar voice responded. It was the Change Agent!

He was standing in the aisle with one hand steering a shopping cart. Handing back the lost package of Jell-O, Mary absently noticed that his shopping cart was filled with nothing but Jell-O!

The Change Agent tossed the Jell-O into the air, and it landed back in his cart after executing a long, graceful arc.

"It's astonishing how losing one thing can lead to gaining something of greater value," he said. "I lost this package of Jell-O to the floor yet gained the rare pleasure of meeting a dear friend."

He continued with a smile. "Do you know the difference," he asked, "between a customer and a client?"

Mary shrugged. "Client sounds fancier?"

The Change Agent chuckled. "Client *does* sound fancier. But there's a very good reason for that.

"Customers are transaction-based. Think of your favorite fast-food burger place. Their customers know what they're getting and are willing to pay for it. It may not be the best hamburger, but, for many, it's worth the money.

"If they were charging twelve dollars for a fancy burger, they probably wouldn't sell as many. They know, and understand, their customer base and what those customers perceive as a value.

"On the other hand, clients are relationship-based. If you have clients, you build a relationship with them, learn what is important to them, and explore ways to enhance that relationship.

"Take the weddings you've done. You spend time with the bride and groom and their families to learn about them as individuals, as a couple, and as a family.

"With that information, you were able to take some amazing pictures that resonated with your clients, and they raved about the work you had done for them. They were very happy and were willing to pay much more than they would for someone else's 'fast-food' version of photography."

He continued, "So, Mary, now that you understand the difference between a customer and a client, what do you want more of... customers, or clients? You may have lost several potential customers this month, yet you gained something ultimately more valuable."

"I want more clients. I want more people I can spend time getting to know and doing high-quality work for," Mary said. But she did have a question to ask. "What have I gained that's more valuable? I'm still waiting for more prospects to come along. I've avoided working with ones that weren't right for me, but I don't see that I've gained anything."

Mary got into the checkout line, the Change Agent following her with his cart full of Jell-O.

"Ah," he said. "That is where you are mistaken. What you've gained are *time* and *energy*. You can use that time and energy to serve more of your ideal clients—who will ultimately pay you more and drain less of your energy.

"Your ideal clients are the people with whom you've built great relationships. They love your work, are your raving fans; they'll pay your prices, whatever you want to charge, within reason.

"These are the people you love working with because they make you happy. With those clients on board, you'll be happier, and you'll make more sales."

"I've never looked at it like that before," Mary said. She was musing over this idea when her cell phone began to ring. She picked up.

Out of the corner of her eye, she noticed the Change Agent examining a box of Jell-O from his cart. With a pleased smile, he casually tossed the box up in the air. Then, another joined. And another. Soon, the Change Agent was merrily juggling half a dozen boxes of Jell-O while the cashier finished with Mary's order.

Whistling, he effortlessly caught the boxes up and placed them, one by one, on the checkout conveyor belt.

When she hung up, it was with a bemused expression on Mary's face that she turned to the Change Agent.

"I never thought of offering photography classes," she said. "But that was what she wanted – the woman I was on the phone with, that is."

"This could be a new silo for you," said the Change Agent. "Most businesses have different silos – in other words, different products that they offer, to different target markets.

"You currently work with clients who need photography for an event or for their business. Teaching photography classes would be a new silo because this new product allows you to appeal to a new target audience – students!

"Therefore, you'll be able to set a new pricing strategy and need to create new marketing messages to fill this silo."

Continuing, the Change Agent said, "To find out if this opportunity could be a profitable new silo for your business, there are five simple questions you need to ask yourself:

1. Is this truly a new silo for you, or does it fall into the same category as one of your other products?

2. Is this new silo offering work that you want to do?

3. What will it cost (in money, time, and effort) for you to deliver what is expected?

4. Do you have the experience and expertise to deliver the desired outcome?

5. What will be the impacts (good and bad) of this new opportunity on your current clients, budget, life, and family?"

"I see," Mary said thoughtfully. "By answering these questions, I'll be able to figure out if this new silo will help me reach my goals."

"Exactly," agreed the Change Agent. "But now, let us move on to a new topic… How are you coming on your 90-day goals?"

Mary replied, "I've accomplished the first three of my 90-day goals. I've been using qualifying questions to screen prospective clients. That's worked great and saved me hours of time that would have been wasted in travel and meeting with people that I would never want to work with!

"I was encouraged by those results, so now I want to identify more ways to stop wasting time and start getting more done."

Mary explained how she had hired a virtual assistant to handle requests for information over email and by phone. To streamline appointment-setting, she hired a freelancer to create a portal that prospective customers could use to set up an appointment through her website.

Before they could book a consultation, the portal required customers to answer her qualification questions in a short survey. This automated a process that used to take hours out of her week.

The Change Agent nodded thoughtfully. "Good work," he said. "Keep an eye out for my message," he added with a wink.

Mary turned around to push her cart out of the store. When she looked behind her again, the Change Agent was gone.

CHAPTER 7

One morning, Mary woke up to find a puzzling note tacked onto her front door. In bold handwriting, it said:

Pour a glass of water onto the sidewalk. At 6 o'clock, we will discuss.

-The Change Agent

Though she had no idea what she'd learn, Mary complied. As she poured the water out of the glass, the stream that fell separated into rivulets of water dripping down the concrete.

Later, frustrated that her washing machine had stopped working, she stopped at the laundromat to put in a quick load of laundry. She was not sure how to find the Change Agent, but she decided he'd find her. Sure enough, the Change Agent arrived at the laundromat at exactly six o'clock.

Unlike her own load, his laundry was composed exclusively of socks of all sizes and colors. His bespoke suit seemed oddly out of context in the harsh lighting of the laundromat.

Without saying hello, he asked, "What did you think of the task you were assigned this morning?"

"I couldn't see the point of it," Mary responded honestly.

"When the water fell, what happened?" he asked.

Seeing that no answers would be forthcoming, Mary thought aloud, "Well, it spread out into uneven trickles across the bumps on the concrete. Some of the water went much further than other trickles, which stopped when it reached a dead end."

"What happened to the water after a couple of minutes passed?" asked the Change Agent.

"It ran out and evaporated," she said.

"Correct!" the Change Agent exclaimed. "You see, the trickles of water are like the referrals from clients you already have. You need more revenue. Instead of investing money in marketing campaigns to get what you need, go for the low-hanging fruit first.

"Ask your current clients to refer you to new clients, or give them the opportunity to buy some other product or service that you offer. These clients already know you and the quality service you deliver. It's really easy for them to buy something else from you or refer someone to you."

Mary grew thoughtful. "I need to give my clients the opportunity to 'pour more water on the concrete,' and make sure I keep the glass full of water. This should result in more clients for my time and energy. Is that the goal?"

"Exactly!" cried the Change Agent. "So you need to...?" He smiled expectantly.

Mary finished his sentence. "Keep asking clients for referrals so that there's a steady stream of new clients, and new business keeps coming in."

"Yes," the Change Agent agreed. "Like referrals, the offshoots formed by the water represent low-effort, high-reward ways to find new sources of revenue. Though investing energy in your business is vital, there are many ways to make more money without actually spending a great deal of money."

"Like what?" Mary asked.

The Change Agent smiled enigmatically as he took a dryer sheet and put it into a sock-stuffed machine. "That is what you are going to tell me! So, let me ask you another question. On average, how much do you make from each client?"

Having already calculated these numbers from her earlier work, Mary was ready with the answers. "High school photography pays $250 per session, but that's only once a year at graduation. Weddings are $1000 a pop, and real estate photography is $200 for three hours of work.

"I have been charging $75 an hour for other miscellaneous jobs like restaurant photography, family photos, and marketing photography for businesses."

"Your recollections serve you well. Now, how could you make more money from these jobs?"

"Well, number one of my 90-day goals was to learn about how to price my work and to recognize how much my time is really worth. When I really looked at the amount of time I was spending on my different silos, I was losing money on real estate work, and just breaking even on most of the things I was doing."

Mary thought for a moment. "Every time I work with a new client, I can offer my other services, like my new photography course or offer to take personal or family portraits. But, what if I could develop an upgraded package that increased a client's value and my revenue at the same time?"

"Imagine the impact if you really could increase your average dollar sale," the Change Agent told her. "You'd make more money and have a better work-life balance because you would work less and juggle fewer clients."

Staring into the rainbow of socks cascading over and over in the tumble dry cycle, he continued, "There are four simple ways you can add more revenue to your business:

Customer referrals that will bring more clients,

Upselling current clients, which will increase average dollar sales,

Offering current clients other services, which will increase the number of transactions, and

Building strategic alliances that will pay off later on."

"Strategic alliances? What are those?" asked Mary.

"A strategic alliance is a relationship with a non-competing business owner. That business should share a common target market, customer or client base with your business.

"When that mutually beneficial connection is made, it turns into a source of revenue over time. For example, this might work well with your friend, Jen, the makeup artist.

"You can talk to your clients about Jen and let them know that she does fantastic makeup for weddings, parties, and major events. If they ever need those services, you know someone who will do a magnificent job. And Jen will promote you to her clients as well, who may well be looking for photography services if they are getting professional makeup done. "Here's another way strategic alliances could work. Let's say you set up a mutual referral agreement with another local service provider. When they send you a new client, they get a commission, and vice versa. Everyone wins," said the Change Agent.

"Who do you know in your network who you would trust and could work with to your mutual benefit? Who has similar target audiences to yours?" the Change Agent asked.

"I can't think of many people," Mary admitted, "but maybe I could find some. There is a florist who uses my services... I know they get clients who are planning weddings, too."

"Excellent," the Change Agent exclaimed. "Think about who you know who serves your ideal type of client and see if you can work out a referral swap." ~~Perhaps you should regularly schedule one such strategic alliance meeting, to ensure that you keep growing?"~~

With a loud buzz, his dryer finished, and his socks stopped tumbling.

He swept up the armful of warm, staticky, multi-colored wool. "I believe yours is done too," he told Mary, moments before her own buzzer went off.

She turned to gather her own clothes, leaning into the warm dryer. When she turned around, she was somehow not surprised that the Change Agent was nowhere to be found.

CHAPTER 8

Monday was a snow day.

Mary's daughter, Eva, was ecstatic. An entire day to watch her favorite shows, all to herself. Mary herself was somewhat less ecstatic, with that adult sensitivity toward the snow piled on her car and the slush-filled streets to navigate.

She called the young man who shoveled snow when he was not in school, only to find that he was all booked up for hours. Mary was forced to don her own coat and grab her snow shovel. Armed thus, she ventured out the front door.

Never had her driveway seemed as large as it did now. A seemingly endless expanse of whiteness stretched before her.

She was shoveling with a vengeance when a familiar voice sounded behind her.

"Allow me."

Mary turned with a relieved smile to see the Change Agent, invariably dressed in a finely tailored suit—though this time with earmuffs.

"Gladly!" she replied. "I didn't expect to see you here."

"So often, we find what we do not expect. How have things gone with your strategic alliance meetings?" the Change Agent asked.

"Oh, yes," Mary replied enthusiastically, setting her shovel to the side. "The first meeting or two was slow. But once everyone got to know each other, and learned to trust each other, the referrals started flowing naturally.

"So far, I've gotten five leads and three new customers from the group. One of the referrals was from the mechanic who comes to our lunches. Turns out his cousin just had a newborn, and he — the cousin — wanted a professional photographer to take pictures of the baby."

"Superb! And the referrals you have been getting, are they your ideal clients?" asked the Change Agent, picking up her shovel.

"I... think so?" said Mary uncertainly.

"To make strategic alliances work well," the Change Agent explained, hefting a shovel full of snow off the driveway, "you'll each need to pay attention to which client experiences give you what you want, and which ones don't. You'll need to build trust and educate each other about your respective business goals. Share the details of how you serve your clients, and the successes and failures you've experienced.

"A big part of the success of a strategic alliance relationship is making sure your alliance partners know what a great referral looks like to you. Then, it is also your responsibility to learn what a great referral is for their business. Learn what is important to them and find ways to add value to the relationship."

The Change Agent paused in his shoveling, though he was not even slightly winded. "Do you know the difference," he asked, "between a lead and a referral?"

Mary shook her head.

"A lead could come in many forms, but it tends to be impersonal and information-based. 'Here is a name of someone that could use your product or service.'

"On the other hand, a referral is someone who has been 'warmed up' by your referral partners. Your referral partner has sung your praises to them and let them know about how great you are.

"Creating a referral-based business takes time, but ultimately it reduces marketing and advertising costs by creating a steady flow of client referrals."

The Change Agent stopped shoveling and asked, "Does that make sense?"

Mary nodded her acknowledgment.

"On another subject—let's talk about Net Profit for your business. Most business owners just hope that this number will be positive. Too many business owners will look at that bottom-line number and make plans to spend it. But I suggest that you divide that number into four equal pieces and put the money in separate accounts with a specific purpose. Those four accounts would be for...

1. Business Reinvestment – money being set aside to purchase future equipment, inventory or supplies.

2. Retained Earnings – this is your 'rainy day' account. Money for you to use if something unexpected happens in the business.

3. Taxes – when you make money, you will pay taxes. Your goal should be to pay as little as possible, but when you write the check, know that it is a milestone that celebrates your success as a business owner.

4. Compensation – use this account to pay yourself and/or your employees.

"Doing things that have a positive impact on your margin percentage will increase your net profit. Some things you can do to increase your margin percentage include:

- Increase your prices

- Sell higher margin products or services

- Stop discounting

- Sell an exclusive label

- Sell to your ideal clients

"These are just some of the ways you can increase your margin percentage!

"I would encourage you to start with the amount of profit you want to make and work backwards to decide what prices you will offer clients.

"When you establish your retail pricing, make sure you include costs for labor, variable and fixed expenses, and net profit."

In a whirlwind of sudden movement, the Change Agent disappeared in a flurry of snow. In a matter of moments, Mary's driveway was shoveled clean and the shovel was neatly back in its place next to her front door.

"How... What..." she was left sputtering as the Change Agent gave a gentle wave, disappearing into the bright winter morning.

CHAPTER 9

Mary frowned at the weed that had sprung up in her garden. Refusing to remove itself from the soil, it stared at her with what she perceived as a defiant expression. She was about to resort to drastic measures when a shadow fell over her plants.

Turning from her gardening, she came face-to-face with the cheerful smile of the Change Agent.

"And to what do I owe this pleasure?" Mary asked with a knowing expression.

"Let's hear an update on your 90-day goals," said the Change Agent. "When we were together last, we talked about your strategic alliance group and improving the quality of referrals that were being shared. How is that going?"

"I shared your thoughts with the group," Mary began, "and they loved the idea. To build understanding and trust, we decided to hold individual one-on-one meetings on weeks between our group meetings. It will take a while to get to meet with all the group members, but we're seeing more trust being built and better-quality referrals being passed. So, we're all seeing better results!"

"That is great news," the Change Agent said, sounding pleased but not surprised. "Congratulations on your success. But you're not done yet!

"When we talked, we also discussed your net profit and what you could do with those funds to help strengthen your business. Have you made any progress?"

"Well," Mary hesitated, "I've started the process. Business has been great, and I'm blessed that there has been profit in the business. I decided to keep a comfortable level of cash in the checking account and move any excess cash out of the business account and put it into another account.

"This keeps working capital in the business and makes me feel more comfortable. The excess is what I'm treating as the net profit, and as the amount grows, I can separate it into the different accounts."

The Change Agent nodded approvingly. "You've made some significant progress over the past few quarters, and now it's time for you to learn how to protect yourself from too much of a good thing—growth!"

"How could growth be a bad thing?" Mary wondered. "All I've ever done is try to grow my business. Now you're telling me to stop?" Her eyebrows crinkled in confusion.

"Not to stop, so to speak, but to control. Explosive business growth so often leads to major problems, while controlled and steady growth will put you on the path to true success. For example, take that tomato plant you are so carefully watering as we speak. Why not pour the whole watering can into the pot?" he asked.

"Too much water would drown this plant. The soil would be saturated, and the roots would rot," Mary replied, trying to keep up with the sudden shift in conversation.

"Correct. Your business, too, has roots. Your business, too, needs water. But too much of a good thing—is not good at all! This is why you must learn to control growth.

"If your business grows too fast, your cash flow won't be able to keep up. So many otherwise solid businesses fall into this trap—they grow as fast as possible, but then find themselves in the throes of a crippling cash flow problem because of the need to spend money on extra equipment, additional space, more inventory or extra labor.

"If you think about it, these things create cash flow and payroll challenges. And we all know how employees react to not getting paid..." The Change Agent trailed off, seemingly recollecting some memory of his own.

After a few moments had passed, Mary prompted, "Yes?"

With a quick shake of his head, the Change Agent adjusted his lapels and continued. "Take this garden. Let us imagine, for a moment, that you have a finite source of water.

"The water is your cash. But with your finite water source, you need to grow your garden. Your garden is your business. The challenge is that if you grow your garden too large, you will not have enough water to feed the rest of your plants, and some of them will die.

"So, how do you allocate your water—your cash flow—to grow your garden while limiting growth to a certain amount, so that you will have exactly enough money to support growth?"

Mary straightened up, then relaxed when she realized the question was rhetorical, not meant for her to answer. Keeping her hands busy, she began weeding and soon developed a calming rhythm.

The Change Agent picked up a stray tomato that had fallen from the vine and rolled it between his fingers. Staring off into the distance as he spoke, he said, "One needs a certain amount of growth, large enough to be significant but small enough to be sustainable. Plan for 20-30% growth per year, and you can avoid many of the problems experienced by some of those high-growth businesses.

"You have already begun growing your business by asking clients for referrals, using your strategic alliance meetings to generate referrals, taking the opportunity to upsell, and screening for your ideal client," he said, popping the tomato into his mouth with a satisfying, juicy crunch. "But now it is time to make sure your growth does not outstrip your capacity. You need to have enough cash flow to support your growth."

"But how, exactly, do I limit growth?" Mary asked.

"How would you do it in your garden?" he rejoined.

"I would plant less seeds so that I had enough water for all of my plants, or I could plant more seeds and thin the weaker plants as they grow to ensure that all the plants that remain will be big and strong," said Mary. "How does this apply to my clients, exactly?"

"You see," said the Change Agent, "your clients are like your plants. If you have less of them, you can limit your business's growth to the 20-30% per year, so that your growth is manageable. Take advantage of this business principal to eliminate some of your customers by screening out those that are less than your ideal clients. You'll get manageable growth and higher-quality clients... Does that make sense?

"And make sure you answer your phone." He winked and vanished around a corner.

"Answer my phone?" Mary wondered aloud. It was not ringing.

CHAPTER 10

Mary and the Change Agent were sitting in the park again, enjoying a sunny day, when the phone rang. Mary picked up.

"Hello? Mhm... Uh huh. Yes. Yes! Really? O-of course! It would be my pleasure." Mary hung up the phone as a smile began to bloom on her face.

"Good news?" he asked.

"Outstanding news!" Mary replied. "I just got a call from a local photographers association. They want me to be the keynote speaker at their annual dinner. The woman on the phone said she kept hearing about my work from her friends, and they want to honor me for my contribution to the local business community." Slightly flustered, she shook her head in faint disbelief.

A beaming smile broke out on the Change Agent's face. "Congratulations! This is superb. I assume you will attend?"

"Of course! I've never been invited to speak before. I feel so honored, and a little scared. Of course, I have no idea what I'll speak about," she laughed.

"You'll figure it out," the Change Agent assured her with a wink.

A few weeks later, Mary had picked out her best outfit for the dinner. She looked in the mirror, took a deep breath, and walked out onto the podium. After her speech, blushing, she descended from the stage.

Between the people she met and the questions she was asked, Mary had no time to think until dinner was served, and everyone went to their tables. Looking down at her plate of grilled salmon, greens, and baby potatoes, she reflected on the last year.

It had started off on a tragic note, her divorce with Ben ripping through the fabric of her life. Issues with her business had grown bigger and bigger as she struggled to find balance between her life and her work.

But then, based on guidance from the Change Agent, she'd made changes in her life and business, which solved each of her problems, one by one.

First, it had been setting goals. Mary chuckled quietly to herself as she remembered how small this had seemed at the time.

Surprisingly, a clear idea of what she needed to do every 90 days and having a 12-month plan made her feel focused and driven. Her goals didn't seem as daunting anymore when broken down into small steps.

Then, it had been getting an understanding of money and how that concept was woven throughout every aspect of her business. She had created a system to screen prospects, and eliminating customers that were a drain on her time and resources was a much bigger relief than she'd expected, both financially and emotionally.

It freed up her energy and time, which was how she was able to take new opportunities when they came knocking.

Utilizing the business financial software allowed her to understand the strength of her growing business. That understanding enabled her to create a growth plan that gave her options she didn't know even existed before.

Tracking weekly KPIs had seemed like a drag at first, but when she started seeing insights that weren't apparent before, she was an instant convert.

Then she figured out ways to get more sales, including upsells, referrals, and regular networking meetings with other professionals. She learned how to prioritize relationships over sales, which, ironically, led to more sales. Finding more of her ideal clients was one of the things that led to more revenue, because her ideal client was happy to pay more for her services.

Crucially, she had curtailed her business's growth to about 25% before too much growth led to insurmountable cash flow problems.

Mary knew that these wouldn't be the last problems she would face in her business. But, for the first time, she believed in her ability to handle them using the techniques she had learned.

After graciously accepting yet more congratulations for her Photography Entrepreneur of the Year Award, and compliments on her speech, Mary left the dinner. In the shadows, she saw a man in a suit.

The Change Agent stepped into the light. "Congratulations, Mary. You did it," he said simply. "For now, our work together is done."

As he spoke those words, he handed her a small velvet bag. "A celebration gift, for achieving a major milestone in your life."

"What? But how will I do this without you? There is so much more to do!" Mary cried. "When I met you, my business was taking over my life. Now, you've helped me solve many of the problems I, and my business, were experiencing, and you've taught me so much more. What will I do when the next problem comes along? What if my business reverts back to the way it was before?" Her newfound confidence was shaken at the news of the Change Agent's departure.

"Impossible!" the Change Agent said adamantly. "Mary, I never solved any of these problems for you. You did it yourself! I shared some insights and helped you think aloud. But you are the only one responsible for your success," he said warmly.

"Besides, I will always be there when you need me. Please, open the gift I just gave you."

She untied the drawstring to open the velvet bag. Inside was an elegantly designed pewter and wood pen that she just knew had to be handmade.

The Change Agent spoke. "This is a special pen. If you ever need me, just use this pen to write the problem you're experiencing down on paper, and I will be there to help. Congratulations, Mary. You have successfully created a mastery of money in your business, and along with that have formed a work-life balance to rival the best of them. Well done!"

He smiled one last time and turned away, whistling to himself as he walked.

Home at last, Mary shut the door behind her and stepped out of her high heels, feeling herself joyfully exhausted as she came down from the excitement of the dinner. With a ring, the backlight on her cell phone sprang to life.

Shocked, Mary stared at her phone. It was Ben! Though Mary had learned how to adapt and react to so many kinds of business challenges, she didn't know what to think. Her ex-husband was calling her after over a year of radio silence.

With trembling fingers, she picked up. A masculine voice on the other line said, "Hello?"

Mary took a deep breath. "Hello, Ben. How are you?" Her tone was deceptively calm. To her surprise, their conversation lingered for over an hour. Though they weren't together, the times they had shared and the relationship they had built were still there.

Mary knew that things would never go back to the way they were. She was a different person. But it was a new beginning.

MARK AND THE DISAPPEARING TIME

CHAPTER 1

Mark winced and pinched the bridge of his nose. But, it didn't help the pounding headache that was throbbing inside his skull. It felt like his brain was trying to get out. And according to his doctor, with his high blood pressure, that was, more or less, what was happening.

Mark wished he could rest. Just go lie down and not worry about business or bookkeeping for a few days. Even a few hours would be nice. But every time he left the office, his phone blew up with calls from the shop.

Doctor Menon said he had to cut back. His blood pressure was dangerous—putting him at increased risk for heart attack and stroke. Mark had almost eliminated salt from his diet, but Menon said that stress was the major factor. But his business was Mark's major source of stress, and there just didn't seem to be any way to cut back on business.

Owning his own business was supposed to be about freedom. That was what Mark had imagined, lying beside his wife at night while he made his plans. He was supposed to have time to spend with Kelly and the kids. He was supposed to be able to set his own hours, take them on vacations, and give them the best of everything.

That was what he'd dreamed of when he partnered in business with his best friend, Scott. When Scott sold his share, allowing Mark to become sole owner, Mark thought Scott was getting the short end of the stick. As full owner, surely Mark would have full control over the business, and his time.

So how did it turn into this?

Mark worked for another hour, pushing through the headache that became blinding and almost made him sick. He knew that was a bad sign, but what could he do? If he let the business go to pot, he wouldn't be able to keep supporting Kelly and the boys!

Finally, Mark rose from his chair. His knees screamed at him. Dr. Menon had said he needed to lose weight for their sake, too — that his back and all his joints were doing too much work with the bending, twisting, and pulling he did at the auto shop.

But how was a working man supposed to get through his long days and nights while on a diet? Mark had never been able to find the time or energy for it, and he didn't think that Dr. Menon was being reasonable.

Kelly liked to point out that Dr. Menon wasn't causing his symptoms — just warning Mark about what *would* happen if he kept this up.

But blaming the doctor was easier than doing what seemed impossible — living a healthy life.

Tonight, Mark was working late for the fifth night this week. 'The office' was now a room in his own home, which he'd thought would be ideal — but it only made it harder to explain to Kelly and the boys why he couldn't spend time with them.

"Can't those invoices wait?" Kelly used to ask.

"I'm sorry, honey, they really can't. They pay our bills, you know?"

When Mark finally finished for the evening, Kelly was still awake and waiting for him in her silk nightgown. He looked at her and wondered where the years had gone. Even in the darkness of the bedroom, she looked much different than the woman he had married.

But — Mark looked down at his own belly — she was doing a whole lot better than him at staying young.

"Hard day?" Kelly asked. It was more a ritual than a real question; the answer was always the same.

"Yeah." He fell into bed beside her, feeling much, much older than he should. He was touched that she'd waited up for him, but knew better than to think she expected more than a few lines of conversation.

Kelly's hand was soft on his arm. The first good thing he'd felt all day. "I'm sorry. I wish I could help."

Mark knew. Kelly wanted to support him, and he wanted to keep supporting her. Why did this seem so impossible?

Kelly rolled over and put on her eye mask. He knew what would follow—he'd pass out, sleep fitfully for a few hours, and then wake up worried around two a.m. He'd check his phone—no messages, of course. You didn't get messages at midnight in the auto repair business unless something had gone really, *really* wrong. But he always checked.

He'd pace around the house for half an hour, an hour—something like that. He joked to Kelly that that was when he got his cardio in, but she didn't seem to find it funny.

He knew she worried herself sick about him. But he didn't know what to do about it.

Kelly used to try to get him to spend more time with the family. "Our boys will only be boys for a little while," she'd say. "You're missing their whole childhood."

"Well, if they want to keep getting their karate lessons, daddy has to work."

Kelly didn't ask Mark to join the family for dinner anymore. She never brought up the fact that it had been—how long? thirteen years?—since she and her husband had a date night. She must have known that if his boys didn't bring him out of the office, nothing would.

She knew now that if he was in his office, he wouldn't come out. He tried to compensate by buying her nicer things, by sending her and the boys on exciting vacations — but he hadn't been able to go on vacation with them in over five years. He just couldn't leave the shop.

Tonight, he closed his eyes for a vacation of a few hours, until the worries woke him up again.

CHAPTER 2

Mark rose before dawn and dressed silently while Kelly slept. She wouldn't be needed at her own job for hours. But he hoped he could get a jump on the day by starting early—maybe he'd even get done in time to have dinner with the family!

Mark had always loved being up before dawn. Something about the early hours of the day even *felt* fresh. The horizon was just beginning to brighten to orange as he took his thermos of coffee and the lunch Kelly packed for him yesterday out to the car. Yes, this was a new day, full of promise.

But as he drove to the shop, he began thinking about what the day ahead would hold. He was going to have to confront Tom, the production manager, about why work was going so slowly on the cars and why orders kept getting bungled.

Why can't I find reliable workers? Mark wondered, thinking angrily of how last week, Amy, his bookkeeper, completely botched an invoice, resulting in a missed payment to a major vendor. *Employees don't care about the company,* he thought. *They just want their paychecks. If I want anything done right, I have to do it myself.*

Mark had tried replacing problem employees, but the replacements he hired all seemed to have the same problems. They were disorganized, couldn't seem to see the big picture, and constantly acted like *they* were under stress despite not seeming to get anything done.

Mark wondered, sometimes, if the life of leisure really did exist. Did those billionaires who owned Walmart really take long, golf course vacations, or were they secretly just as busy trying to make their companies work as he was?

His mind then turned to Kelly and his sons — the reason he started the business to begin with. Ethan was eleven now — new to middle school and doing great, and in soccer and karate. Jacob was nine, and making his mother proud by bringing home straight As.

But Mark couldn't remember the last time he spent quality time with either of them, outside of church on Sundays. And they didn't seem to appreciate how hard it was to make money. He hated the resentful looks Ethan was beginning to give him as he approached his teenage years. He hated having to turn down Jacob's insistent requests that Mark practice baseball with him.

He would have loved to do those things. But he didn't have time.

Before long, a pounding headache began to blossom. It seemed to rise with the sun, and soon the sun was hurting his eyes as he drove into it toward the shop on the east side of town.

Wincing, not trusting himself to see through the blinding pain, Mark pulled the car over to the side of the road with a slight squeak of tires and watched the traffic pass him by.

Great. Now he was going to be late.

He leaned against his steering wheel, wincing. *What is wrong with me?*

He'd thought his old partner was losing out when he offered to sell Mark his portion of the business. But now, Mark was beginning to wonder if Scott knew something he didn't. He wondered what Scott was doing right now…

And then Mark jumped at a sharp rapping on his driver's side window.

"Excuse me," a voice came, muffled, through the glass. "But it looks to me like you may be in need of assistance."

Mark looked up, frowning. The stranger had said that as a statement more than as a question. He said it as if he meant more than just the car.

"I'm fine, thanks," Mark retorted, rolling down his window so the guy could see he was alright. The last thing he needed was to get the cops called on him on the way to work. But as he looked the stranger up and down, Mark's frown only deepened.

There was something *odd* about this fellow. He didn't look like a harried passerby who had taken time out of his busy morning to check on a stranger. He was wearing a clearly expensive tailored suit, and there was something a little old-fashioned about his outfit and demeanor. More than that, he looked like someone who *meant* to be there. Almost like he had an appointment.

"Who are you?" Mark asked.

"I," the stranger said, pulling a card from his suit pocket with a slight flourish, "am known as the Change Agent. I help people just like you to create the businesses you want."

Mark blinked, staring at the business card that was presented to him. The man seemed serious. "Well, you've got a hell of a marketing strategy. How did you find me?" he asked in disbelief.

"Uh, uh." The Change Agent wagged his finger. "You'll find this easier if you don't question my methods." He leaned forward, propping his elbows casually on the window sill of Mark's car. "Now tell me — is it true that you've been having a rough time with your business?"

"I — well. Yes." Mark was suddenly suspicious. "Who told you?"

"You did, good sir. It's written all over your face."

Mark raised an eyebrow.

"Now — do you want a way out of your trouble?"

"I'm not selling," Mark growled.

"Well, that's good," the Agent said amicably, "because I'm not buying. I am here to help you with the problem of your missing time."

That got Mark's full attention. "I'm listening."

"Before we begin," the Agent started, "there are two questions you must answer for me."

Mark waited.

"Do you want to grow your business?"

"I don't see how I can. Managing what we've got already is... too much," Mark admitted. "I've been thinking about cutting back."

"That's not what I asked," the Agent said sternly. "I asked if you *want* to grow your business. Not whether you think you *can*."

"Well, of course I *want* to —"

"Do you *really* want to?"

"Yes!" This Change Agent guy was starting to get under Mark's skin.

The Agent gave a satisfied nod. "Very good. Now, this one's tougher — are you willing to change the way you do things?"

Mark frowned. "I don't see how that's—"

"Just answer the question! Are you willing to change the way you do things—*if* it will fix your problem?"

"I—" Mark would give just about anything for more time with Kelly and the kids. "Fine. Yes. I am *willing* to change the way I do things."

The Change Agent clapped his hands together, looking delighted. "Good! Then you have everything you need to achieve your goals!"

"I don't see *how!*"

"You will." The Change Agent pulled an ancient-looking flip phone from his pocket, flipped it open, and smiled. "Ah, excellent. Kelly will be joining us at the shop over her lunch break."

Mark stared, bewildered. "... *how?*"

"Just doing my job," the Change Agent smiled. "Now, get moving! Or you'll be late."

And then the man was *gone*. Mark looked around frantically, wondering how he'd slipped out of sight. There was nothing left but Mark and the morning traffic.

As he pulled back out into it, Mark realized that his headache was gone.

# #

The morning went about as well as Mark had expected. Tom tried to blame everyone else in sight for the production delays and the paperwork problems that surfaced last week. He even tried to blame *Mark*, insisting that Mark had gotten documents to him late.

Mark considered firing him on the spot—and would have, if he hadn't dreaded the prospect of spending months training a new manager who wouldn't know anything about how the shop worked. Mark settled for giving him a stern reprimand and taking a generous dose of aspirin.

Come lunchtime, Mark hadn't been planning to sit down. He had planned to take inventory himself—since his employees apparently couldn't be trusted to do it—when he ran into an unexpected obstacle.

There was a hand on his bagged lunch.

He looked up and saw that the hand belonged to the Change Agent, who was smiling at him expectantly. "Kelly's here," the Agent said.

Mark began to panic. If Kelly was here to have lunch, then who was going to do inventory…

His panic evaporated when Kelly appeared in the doorway. He had forgotten how *beautiful* she was.

The Change Agent gestured, still smiling, for Mark and Kelly to follow him to the lunchroom in the back of the shop where they could have some privacy.

Mark felt almost shy as they both pulled out bags containing sandwiches, like school kids.

It felt almost like a *date*.

"Mark, Kelly," the Change Agent began, pulling up a folding chair in front of them, "thank you for meeting me here today. I've already explained to both of you what I do... I help business owners make their business all that they want it to be."

Kelly nodded, looking hopeful. Mark eyed her, sidelong. He'd have to ask Kelly where she found this 'Change Agent' guy.

"Every business owner is different," the Change Agent continued. "But there are two things all *successful* business owners have in common:

1. Desire to grow their business

2. Willingness to change what they're doing

"I believe we've confirmed that both of you have both of those things. Correct?"

Kelly nodded eagerly. Mark followed suit.

"Now, Mark," the Change Agent began, addressing him seriously, "I have one more question for you: Why isn't your business doing what you want it to do?"

Mark looked at the Change Agent. He looked at Kelly. He opened and closed his mouth silently.

A few hours ago, he had countless answers—all the things he could not change. But now as he reflected on it, he wasn't sure. Other people were having successful businesses. Why wasn't he?

"The answer," the Change Agent supplied gently, "is that every business is a direct reflection of its owner. The good, the bad, and the ugly."

He continued, "If the owner is disorganized, the business will be, too. If the owner is selfish, it will reflect in the employees. If the business owner lives in chaos and drama, those things will find their way into their business, and the result is never positive."

Mark felt his face beginning to go red, and a pounding headache starting. "Now, see here! If you think I'm *selfish*—" he began. But then Kelly's hand was on his arm.

The Change Agent held his hand up solemnly. "That was only an example. These are not accusations, just one of the universal truths. We don't know what the issues are within your business, yet. But, what I do know is that you are putting a great deal of time, effort and energy into your business—and you are not seeing the results you want. Do you want that to continue?"

"I—no," Mark admitted.

Kelly looked thoughtful. "You told me," she said to the Change Agent, "that you could help Mark reach his goals. Growing his business—that doesn't mean he'll need to spend *more* time working, does it?"

"Absolutely not," the Change Agent confirmed. "In fact, after we've identified the roots of Mark's disappearing time, he will have more time—and more customers—than ever before!"

"I don't see how that's possible," grouched Mark.

"Well," the Change Agent said, "allow me to attempt to change your mind. My first step must be to have confidential thirty-minute interviews with each of your team members. I must discover where *they* feel the challenges exist."

"I ask them that all the time!" Mark exploded. "They just tell me—"

"Ah, yes." The Change Agent cut him off with a hand gesture again. "But they may be afraid to tell you the truth. You sign their paychecks, after all. If you think you already know the cause of the problems, they may be afraid to contradict you—even if they know something you don't!"

Mark considered this. He *had* been told he could come across as intimidating...

"Mark," the Change Agent said, "you have your perspective of your business, and each of your employees sees things from their own perspective. Just like looking at the same object from different angles, each perspective contains different information. And you can get the most complete picture by looking at *all* the perspectives and putting together the information they contain.

"My objective is to get information from all those perspectives — snapshots of your business from every angle, if you will. Then, and only then, will we be able to identify — and fix, if needed — all of its moving parts."

Mark found himself frowning, but not in anger. That made a surprising amount of sense!

"It may also be that your workers themselves do not know why they are struggling, and that they need to be asked the right questions," the Change Agent continued. "With your permission, I will ask each of your employees these questions:

1. What do you like about working with Mark?

2. What don't you like about working with Mark?

3. What are five things Mark could do or provide that would improve your attitude, productivity or performance?

4. If there was ONE thing that needed to be done to improve the business, what would it be?"

Mark's curiosity was piqued. "Alright," he agreed. "I guess I'll need to set up appointments for you…"

"No need to spend your time on that," the Change Agent said brightly. "I will take care of it, but would you mind if Amy shared with me your business's financial reports from the past years?"

What did Mark have to lose? "Sure," he responded. "That would be fine."

The Change Agent continued, "Thank you! Now, there's one more thing that both of you can do to prepare for our next meeting."

Kelly and Mark looked at each other.

"Have you ever heard the term 'Big Rocks'?"

They both looked back to the Change Agent, frowning.

"Your Big Rocks are the really important things in your life that you want to make room for, before you schedule anything else.

"Mark, for you, they might be things like Kelly and your boys, your faith, and personal time for you to get healthy. Kelly—I imagine your priorities are similar. But I want each of you to determine what your *Big Rocks* are before we meet again.

"Imagine, if you will," the Change Agent continued, "a large bowl filled with five big rocks. This bowl represents the time we all have in our lives. The universe hates a vacuum — if we do not choose our Big Rocks and put them in the bowl first, the universe will fill it with whatever sorts of tasks happen to fall in. Soon, our lives are taken up by all sorts of things we would not have chosen if we'd thought about it, like meetings, paperwork, upset customers, vendors, unwanted phone calls, distractions, etc.

"By *choosing* our Big Rocks, we take control of our time. It's no longer filled by whatever tasks just happen to fall into our lives."

Mark stopped suddenly and stared. From somewhere, the Change Agent had produced an *actual* glass fish bowl, into which he plunked five large pieces of colored plastic — the Big Rocks, he assumed. Then he began to pour marbles around the Big Rocks, then some sand — and eventually the bowl was filled to the brim.

"Now," the Change Agent explained, "the time in this life has all been filled by tasks — the marbles and sand. But if you hadn't put the Big Rocks in first, how would you be able to fit them in?"

Kelly looked at Mark thoughtfully, and Mark felt his face burning. Had he failed to make room for Kelly and his boys? How much more time did he have left to fill?

Mark looked back at the Change Agent. "As a business owner, I often feel like I'm not getting enough done. Now here you are telling me that I need to get less done — to get more done? How does that make sense?"

The Change Agent chuckled quietly, murmuring to himself something that sounded suspiciously like *That's what they all say.*

"You need," he said at full volume for Mark and Kelly to hear, "to identify what your Big Rocks are. They're different for everyone, but equally vital to us all. Our Big Rocks are, in a very real sense, why we are here.

"When you have your list of Big Rocks, let's get together and you can share them with me. Then, I will share the results of the employee interviews… How about dinner, day after tomorrow?"

And then Kelly's hand was on Mark's, over his sandwich. "I guess," she said, "that gives us a few minutes together now."

And for the first time in years, Mark felt himself blushing.

CHAPTER 3

Kelly was wearing a dress Mark hadn't seen on her in ten years. She'd once told him that she was 'too old for it now.' Mark wondered if the Change Agent had had a talk with her about that, too.

The dress was working for her really, really well.

She had already ordered a ceviche appetizer for them when Mark and the Change Agent rolled into the expensive restaurant. When the waiter came, they placed their orders. Kelly selected lobster thermidor, Mark chose his favorite lamb vindaloo, while the Change Agent opted for a vegetable dish.

"Delicate stomach," he explained, patting his belly as the server brought their appetizer.

"So," Mark coughed, tearing his attention away from Kelly. "What was it you wanted to talk to me about?"

The Change Agent steepled his fingers and looked from Kelly to Mark. "Have you two thought about your Big Rocks since we last spoke?"

Mark nodded, feeling absurdly like a schoolboy turning in homework. "My Big Rocks are... here." He withdrew a folded piece of paper from his pocket and handed it to the Change Agent. The list read:

1. To be a great father and husband (!!!)

2. To get healthy

3. To have a true business

The Change Agent seemed a bit amused as he looked Mark's list over. "Mark," he asked, "could you tell me what a 'true business' means to you?"

Mark smiled, a little proud of himself. "I read this definition in a business magazine this week, and really liked it. They said a true business is 'a commercial, profitable enterprise that works even without the owner.'"

The Change Agent nodded thoughtfully. "Now — what does 'being a great father and husband' mean to you?"

Mark looked fondly at Kelly next to him. "It means being able to spend quality time with my boys and Kelly and support them emotionally *as well as* financially."

The Change Agent thought about this for a long moment — or perhaps he was just letting Kelly and Mark think! Finally, he asked gently, "If that is your number-one most important Big Rock, what's been keeping you from doing it?"

To Mark's great surprise, his eyes burned. He felt tears welling up. How long had it been since he'd cried — even in front of Kelly? "The business is taking all my time — and my life..." he managed. "And I don't know how to stop it."

The Change Agent queried, "In a perfect world, how much time would you like to work in your business?"

"Right now," Mark said, "I'd be happy if I could have dinner with the family each night, maybe spend five or six hours each week doing that. I'd love to be able to do that *and* attend the boys' sporting activities, and take them on vacation..."

"Great!" the Change Agent exclaimed. "That's a great goal. Let's start with dinner time and see how that goes! Now," the Change Agent consulted Mark's list again, "how about your desire to get healthy? What are you doing to achieve that now?"

Mark felt himself blushing again. "Nothing," he admitted. He could feel Kelly's eyes on him.

The Change Agent smiled. "It's okay, we all have to start making changes somewhere. How would it look for you to get started?"

Mark hesitated. If he said something now, in front of Kelly, he figured he'd have to actually do it. That was surprisingly intimidating! "Dr. Menon suggested that I walk about one mile, three times per week. I think I could start there," Mark decided.

The Change Agent nodded approvingly. "Great. Which three days would make sense for your work schedule?"

Mark frowned. No day was a *good* day to take time away from the office… "I'm not sure," he confessed. "But I think Tuesday, Thursday and Saturday mornings would be easiest."

"Wonderful!" the Change Agent said brightly. "Now, on to your final Big Rock. You desire to have a True Business. I understand the definition, but you should know that this, much like improving your health, will take time. It does not happen overnight. But it will happen, if you take the necessary steps!"

Mark nodded resolutely. "I understand," he declared. "If I'm gonna do this, then let's reach for the stars!"

The Change Agent smiled. "Very well. Let's work together to make that happen! First step — do you use a calendar?"

"Sure," Mark responded. "At the shop, to schedule customers."

"Why do you do that?" the Change Agent asked.

Mark blinked. "To make sure we know we will have time for every customer that schedules an appointment, of course. We can't just expect to remember each appointment we have!"

"Then," the Change Agent suggested, "why aren't you doing the same thing in your personal life?"

Mark blinked again.

"I suggest you keep a personal calendar. It can be a hard copy or on your phone. But I encourage you to put all these Big Rocks in your calendar and treat these events with the level of importance that you would treat an important customer meeting. If your work engagements are important enough for a calendar, why aren't your personal engagements?

"When you do this," the Change Agent explained, "you'll make sure you invest your time in those things that are really important to you. Once you learn how to manage your own time wisely, you will be able to increase your quality of life and improve your relationships with family and friends.

"And because you'll know that you're investing your time in the things that are most important to you, you'll feel better about yourself and your business."

The Change Agent smiled. "I look forward to seeing your personal calendar when we meet next! Now, on to another subject. What *is* time?"

Mark turned and looked at the Change Agent in surprise. This philosophical question hardly seemed to have a place in a business meeting. "It's…" He concentrated, remembering his high school physics classes. "Part of the fabric of the universe?" he recited.

"Very good! Time," the Change Agent said, "is the fabric of our lives."

That sounded like something Mark could understand.

"We are all given the same amount of time," the Change Agent explained. "Sixty minutes in an hour, twenty-four hours in a day, seven days in a week, three hundred and sixty-five days in a year. This is the material we are given with which to craft our lives; it's the things we fill our time with that shape our self-esteem, and our vision of ourselves as business owners, spouses, parents, and any other role we may wish to undertake."

Mark thought about this.

"When we do the same thing for a long time," the Change Agent continued, "we feel like time is passing very fast. We may not even notice as the years of our lives pass us by! But when we pay close attention to how we invest our time and change it according to our needs—time seems to pass much more slowly. How do you feel about the last few years, Mark?"

Mark reflected. "I haven't felt like I *had* a choice about what I was doing. I'm still not sure I do. But you seem pretty confident about it!"

"You feel as though you don't have control, because you were operating based on old ideas — things that worked at one time, but don't work for you any longer.

"You weren't continuously assessing your needs. Once, you needed to worry about not having enough customers; once, you needed to worry about cutting costs. Now you need to focus on the most important thing... investing your time where it is most important.

"Now, Mark, Kelly," the Change Agent continued, "Mark's employees have told me some very interesting things. Based on what I heard, I am more confident than ever that I can help you."

The Change Agent withdrew some papers written in flowing, graceful script from his pocket. "It is my understanding that you have owned this business for... eleven years?"

Mark nodded.

"And you were originally partners with a Scott, is that right?"

Mark nodded again.

The Change Agent leaned back in his chair. "What happened there?"

Mark shrugged. "I... didn't like the way Scott was doing things. I didn't think the things he was doing were good for business. So, we talked it over and he sold me his share."

The Change Agent nodded thoughtfully and looked back at his notes, knowing that it could not have been that simple and easy, but not sure whether it was worth digging deeper.

"Well, your employees say that you're an excellent mechanic. Your numbers say it, too. I see that your revenue has been rising steadily every year since Scott left. And your customers all seem to come back! That's commendable. But it has resulted in the workload becoming too big for you and Bill to do alone, hasn't it?"

Mark nodded reluctantly. "Yeah, but I just can't seem to find good help."

"Mm," the Change Agent hummed. "Might I suggest that you are very good with cars—but perhaps not the best judge of people?"

Mark bristled.

"I see that your shop has the capacity for four mechanics, for example—but you only have two. Why is that?"

"Well," Mark hesitated. "Bill—he's the other mechanic, other than me—he doesn't get along so well with everyone. He already has trouble getting work done while I'm not around, and I didn't want to make it worse by giving him someone to fight with."

"The way you fought with Scott?" the Change Agent suggested.

Mark winced. "Well... maybe."

"I hear that you've let several mechanics go in the past as well. Is that true?"

"I... yeah."

"Why was that?"

"They weren't doing what I wanted," Mark responded indignantly. "Everybody's got their own ideas about how to do this job — and mine's obviously the one that works. The numbers show that! You just said so yourself."

The Change Agent nodded thoughtfully. "Yes. Customers like your work. But, it would seem that it's coming with a cost. Do *you* like your quality of life?"

"I... no."

"Then perhaps it is time to find a way to both keep your customers happy and improve your own quality of life."

Mark frowned.

"It's not that keeping customers happy is a bad thing, or even an optional thing," the Change Agent explained. "But some business owners have such particular ideas about how to do that, they have trouble delegating work to others. That guarantees that you do everything yourself — even things that others could do easily."

Mark nodded grudgingly.

"It certainly seems," the Change Agent offered, "that you do not have a shortage of customers. I see here that your revenue grew last year. But Kelly tells me that you are working eighty-hour weeks to make sure everything is done exactly the way you'd like. She is afraid of what will happen to you if the business grows any more without some serious changes!"

"I don't blame her," Mark muttered.

He looked at Kelly. He didn't have to guess why she wasn't saying much: She'd already told him her thoughts many times, and he had more or less ignored them. Maybe the Change Agent would be able to give him the know-how to make Kelly's suggestions seem possible.

"Now," the Change Agent began, "what is the future you would *like* to see?"

Mark thought about it. He'd been daydreaming for years of a world where he would have enough time to take long vacations with Kelly and the boys. He pictured all four of them together on a white, sandy beach—or even at Ethan's Saturday soccer games!

"I want to have more time with my family," Mark said. "Like, a lot more time."

"How many hours per week would you be working—if you could choose?"

"Thirty!" Mark blurted. Yes. Six-hour days with weekends off would be just perfect.

"I think we can arrange that," said the Change Agent, smiling.

Mark narrowed his eyes. "What do you mean, 'we?'"

"Well, it will mostly be you," explained the Agent. "You will be making all the changes to make it happen. But I do have some rather extensive experience in this area. I will be able to supply you with... helpful insights and nudges, from time to time."

Mark crossed his arms. It sounded good... too good.

"The next thing we must do," said the Agent, "is decide what changes you will make in the next ninety days to get closer to your goal. What do you think those might be?"

Mark took a deep breath. "Well, two things come to mind... First, I need to hire two new mechanics — but my history in that area has not been good. Second, it would be great if Tom would take responsibility for all customer service and Amy actually handled all the bills and invoices."

"Why do you think they don't right now?"

Mark hesitated. "Well... what did they tell you?"

The Change Agent looked suddenly very serious. "Amy mentioned that it can be difficult for her to keep track of what she is supposed to be doing, because you're frequently changing the way you want things done. She also mentioned that there are no systems or procedure manuals for everyone to follow, and no contact database of customers. Tom feels like you micromanage him and never appreciate what he does for the business."

Mark pinched the bridge of his nose. "Yeah," he tapped his head, "it's all in here. I haven't found anyone I would trust with the vendor pricing, supplier details and my customer list. So, I keep these things in my head. Not real smart, huh?" Mark continued, "Back when I worked with Scott, I got better results than anyone else working with vendors... so I guess I still like working with them."

The Change Agent leaned forward. "Don't you think that might be costing you quite a lot of time?"

"Well... I guess. But it saves money."

"Lack of revenue does not seem to be a problem for you."

"I guess," Mark admitted reluctantly.

"In the next few weeks," the Change Agent said, standing, "I invite you to consider what changes you need to make — personally, and professionally.

"We've talked about your Big Rocks and how important those things are to you. Now you need to combine those things and take a serious look at your personal and business life, and how you want it to change.

"Ask yourself what you need to *start, change* and *stop*. Make a list of goals that you want to accomplish in the next ninety days, both in terms of your business and your personal life. In time," the Change Agent's eyes twinkled, "we will even create one-year and three-year plans for you. Do you think you can do that, Mark?"

Mark nodded reluctantly.

The Change Agent bowed slightly. "Thank you," he said, "for a wonderful meal and enlightening conversation. Now I'll leave the two of you to enjoy the rest of your date."

With a wink, the Change Agent strode away, whistling.

CHAPTER 4

Over the next week, Mark created his personal calendar. Though he was anxious about it at first, he soon saw the value in making sure his Big Rocks were scheduled into his day. He was hoping to spend a few hours each week having dinner with his family or following his doctor's advice. If things went as planned, nothing would fall apart at the shop because of it!

There were some bumps in the road. Sometimes he underestimated the amount of time he'd need to spend traveling to and from events, like his son's soccer games, and ended up behind. A few important business projects *did* fall behind schedule—but Mark found himself feeling a little bit of hope that the Change Agent could help him fix these.

A few things did not change. He still needed to do a lot of work on cars around the shop, despite assigning some of them to Bill and hiring Jimmy, a local high school student who wanted to work on cars.

Mark needed *time*. The Change Agent was right—he *didn't* need more customers or lower costs. And the only way to get more time was to get more employees.

Mark placed ads and started asking people if they knew any good mechanics that might be looking for a change. He was happy that the responses from potential candidates came so quickly.

Some of his candidates were new and had no job experience at all. They said they knew all the latest techniques from their education—but he had nothing to go on as far as their work experience.

Others were veteran mechanics who had worked for other auto shops, but they came with their own sets of concerns. Why had they left their old jobs? What if they were accustomed to doing things a certain way, and couldn't adjust to the way Mark did things?

Mark had encountered both problems with past employees, and he had never been able to solve them. He always ended up simply firing the new employees, leaving him with only Bill for help. But with the Change Agent's promise of help, Mark hoped things would go differently this time.

Mark started interviewing new mechanics—and this time, tried to make his hiring decisions based on their ability to do some basic jobs. He created a basic skills test to see if the prospective employees could do expected tasks. He didn't judge whether they did it 'his way'—if the quality of work was there and the time spent was reasonable, he figured, they could be a good fit to help him serve his customers.

Of the nine mechanics he interviewed, Mark found two that he thought might work very well.

As part of the interview process, Mark followed the Change Agent's suggestion and had Bill and Tom be part of the second interview. This way they could provide their insights, and, hopefully, take some responsibility for making sure the two new mechanics worked out.

He agreed to let Jimmy move up to half-time as the school year let out. He made Amy's database and delivered it into her delighted hands.

Mark was busier for a little while, double-checking Amy's work, making sure Tom was on track with working the new mechanics into the production schedule, and looking over Jimmy's work to make sure it was getting done, and then...

And then, he was less busy.

The invoices, inventory, and orders started to get done on time.

Now, with increased capacity from the new mechanics, Tom was able to get customer vehicles serviced faster. Mark waited for the customer complaints to start rolling in... that repairs were late, or that cars were falling apart—but they didn't come.

Amy had begun to handle the invoicing and paperwork over the last few weeks, and Mark was expecting to hear from vendors that hadn't been paid—but those calls never came!

There was a problem, though. Bill's role as senior mechanic was to work closely with the new mechanics, Jeff and Howard.

Bill was also in charge of training Jimmy, and with a junior mechanic learning under him, Bill started to seem full of himself and bossy when Mark went into the shop.

More than once, Mark found Bill yelling at Jimmy. Mark always stepped in when he saw that happening, knowing it was his responsibility to protect new employees. But it kept happening.

But even so, Mark found that the business was running much smoother than he'd ever expected.

#

He was able to leave the shop—*early*—one Friday. Mark surprised Kelly by coming home for family dinner.

His boys were surprised too. And delighted.

"Dad, dad!" Jacob clamored as he jumped up, ran past Mark, and disappeared.

"Some enthusiasm," Mark murmured, watching his son. But, Jacob reappeared a moment later waving a framed certificate.

"I made the honor roll!" he proclaimed, shoving the certificate into Mark's hands. Mark found himself laughing.

Over the table, Kelly smiled.

"We should do this more often," she commented.

"Yes," Mark agreed. "We should." And he smiled.

Later that evening, after the boys were in bed, Mark thought about the Change Agent's assignment for him.

Mark had been skeptical about the benefit of writing down any of his plans. He hadn't yet finished his list of 90-day goals, working on them a little at a time as they came to him.

But Mark had to admit, what he was doing, so far, seemed to be *working*. He pulled out the list of 90-day goals and studied them.

90-day plan

1. Hire at least two mechanics to increase capacity

2. Find out what Tom, Amy and Bill are doing

3. Make it home for dinner once a week

4. Find time to work out

As Mark looked at this list and realized he'd made progress on almost everything on it, he wondered: What could he do with a one-year and a three-year plan?

# #

Mark had time this morning. Enough time to stop on a park bench on his way to work and think. He sat by the lazy local river and imagined where he wanted to be three years from now.

On a beach. With Kelly. Ethan would be in high school by then—and probably interested in girls, Mark thought, chuckling to himself. Jacob would be in middle school.

He was somehow not surprised when a tall, slender man in a finely tailored suit appeared around the other side of the bench.

"May I?" The Change Agent gestured to the empty seat.

"Please."

The Change Agent sat for a moment, looking at the water. "So," he asked Mark, "how are you feeling now?"

"Good," Mark enthused. "I've been delegating more—and nothing has gone wrong. I've also started walking three times per week and met a trainer at the gym. I like him! I think he can help me."

The Change Agent smiled. "Congratulations on scheduling regular exercise. Your health is invaluable! It's also great that you're learning to trust your people. Just because you are very good at what you do," the Change Agent explained, "does not mean that other people aren't as good, or better."

Mark nodded sagely. "I've been thinking," he said slowly, "about my one and three-year plans."

The Change Agent waited expectantly.

"I think," Mark said, "that if this year continues to go well, and the *two* mechanics work out, I'd like to stop doing production altogether. As it is, I just fill in when Tom needs help. If that happens, then all I'll have to do is work with the vendors."

The Change Agent nodded approvingly.

"And if that goes well—I might open a second location."

The Change Agent smiled. "If that works out, what will happen to your business?"

"Well," Mark said, "if everything goes as I expect, business will continue to grow and I could probably work half-time."

The Change Agent nodded approvingly again. "And why," he asked, "do you *want* to do that?"

Mark paused. He wanted to say, 'to spend time with Kelly and the kids,' but something about that answer seemed incomplete. He tried again. "Because... I want to choose how I spend my time."

"Business owners like you," the Change Agent bowed, "can make the best use of time by careful evaluation and planning. When that happens, you'll invest your time doing exactly what will help you achieve your plans—and nothing else! Keep your short- and long-term plan in mind as you create your SMART goals."

"SMART goals?" Mark replied, questioning and slightly irritated. Was the Change Agent saying his goals weren't smart?

"The best way to reach your goals," the Change Agent announced with a flourish, "is to create SMART goals. You see, SMART is an acronym! It stands for

Specific

Measurable

Achievable

Results-focused

Time-bound

"SMART goals will help you find concrete, measurable steps to reach your longer-term plans. When setting up SMART goals, ask yourself...

"Who is going to do What by When?

"If you write each goal to answer those questions and follow through on meeting your self-imposed deadlines—it is almost impossible to fail!"

"Well, I'm plenty smart—" Mark started.

"Yes, Mark, you are," the Change Agent agreed. "If your goal is specific, your progress toward it can be concretely measured, is within the realm of what you can really do, and you establish a fair timeline for completion—there is almost no way you will not reach that goal," the Change Agent repeated.

Mark thought about this. He'd never been big on fancy formulas or acronyms—but maybe that was why he was in so much trouble now!

"The best way to form goals," the Change Agent continued, "is to work backwards. Figure out what your long-term goal is, then work backwards to make a 12-month plan towards achieving that."

"Well, to make this a SMART goal, I want to be working no more than thirty hours a week twelve months from today," Mark said, although this goal seemed impossible.

"Very good," said the Change Agent. "That is specific, measurable, and achievable. It is something that will help you get the *result* of not having to spend as much of your time on office tasks. And it is time-bound—you can give yourself a deadline!

"So, what could you do to make that SMART goal possible?"

"Well," Mark pondered, "hiring the two mechanics was a great start. Now I could... trust Tom and Amy to do more of the work that has been bogging me down? Yeah. Those two things could free up a big chunk of my time—maybe fifteen or twenty hours per week!"

"Wonderful goals. But there are a few things that need to be accomplished before you can reach that point," the Change Agent said gently. "In the next few months, I will show you the important steps to create the culture of a workplace that really works for you!"

The Change Agent walked with Mark back to the parking lot.

Mark wasn't surprised when the Change Agent said, "I have a new assignment for you, Mark. There are a few proven principles, practices, tools, and techniques that can help you use your time to achieve your goals—and to focus on nothing else.

"I will talk to you about the first of these practices soon. In the meantime, please rewrite your 90-day plan to ensure that they are SMART goals. Determine precisely when you will do the work needed to make them happen and give yourself deadlines."

The Change Agent continued. "There will be one more crucial piece to your success. Remember how we discussed seeing an object—or a business—from every angle, to identify all its moving parts?

"Ask each of your employees to write down what tasks they perform for the business every hour, day, week, month, quarter, semi-annually, annually and as needed. By comparing these lists, you will find some things that are being duplicated, and you may find out that some things aren't being done at all.

"Does that make sense? Do you understand the assignment?"

"Yeah," Mark agreed. "I can't make sure things get done efficiently if I don't know *what's* currently getting done."

The Change Agent smiled. "Very good. Now if you'll excuse me, I have ducks to feed!"

The Change Agent stood up, producing a loaf of bread from *somewhere*. Mark had stopped questioning where the Change Agent kept his arsenal of odd objects.

The mysterious man strode away along the river, whistling.

Mark looked at his watch. It was time to get back to work.

CHAPTER 5

In the next few weeks, Mark was making some progress, but seemed to keep hitting potholes on his path to managing his time. He had been able to continue his workouts three times a week, and his trainer was keeping him focused on his progress. But some of the same old problems began surfacing with his new mechanics, Jeff and Howard.

Tom reported that they had been coming in late, and he had noticed that there were signs that the quality of work was dropping. Mark was concerned that he would have to let them go, just like so many others. But there had to be a way to fix this—didn't there?

Tom was really stepping up in his role as primary customer contact. He was the first contact the customer had with the shop and the last person to see them as they left. His role was vitally important, and he was doing great. But Mark also needed him to help make sure the new mechanics were doing what they were supposed to be doing, and not learning the bad habits that Bill might be teaching them.

And Bill—Bill seemed to be doing as little work as ever. Amy told Mark that she heard him treating the new mechanics in a way that made her feel uncomfortable.

Mark was working less—sixty hours now, instead of seventy or eighty. He'd freed up Saturdays and Sundays for the boys' activities, which had Kelly ecstatic. But he still found himself staying through dinner at the shop more than he wanted, as he picked up the slack Bill wasn't handling.

One day as he was leaving the shop, walking out into a late summer sunset, Mark was relieved to see the slender form of the Change Agent standing by his car.

"Mark!" The Agent greeted him with an enthusiastic handshake.

"I wanted to come see you. Kelly called me in tears yesterday to share some amazing news... she told me that for the last few nights, you've slept through the night. Congratulations, and well done!"

Mark smiled. "Yeah, I was surprised as well. It felt good to get a good night's sleep!"

The Change Agent looked delighted. "So, how has your business been?"

Mark leaned against his car, hesitating. "It's been... good. I have more time. But not as much as I'd like."

The Change Agent waited respectfully.

Mark sighed. "Truth be told, I'm having the same problems I've always had. Some of the employees aren't doing their jobs—

not all of them, anyway. And I'm not sure what to do about it 'cause I'm afraid the same thing will happen again."

The Change Agent nodded. "Which employees are you having trouble with?"

"Tom, Amy, and Jimmy are doing great. But the new mechanics—not so much. I'm worried that Bill may be a bad influence on them."

"Oh my," the Change Agent murmured, "a senior member of your business, a bad influence? That *is* distressing. What are you seeing?"

Mark sighed. "I asked Bill to mentor the new mechanics— kind of show them the ropes, answer questions, help them feel comfortable working here. But I see him treating Jeff and Howard like he's their boss. Telling them what to do, demanding that they change the way they do things, and talking down to them.

"And I asked him to train Jimmy to do some of the simple work around the shop, like doing oil-changes or changing a tire, but I've caught him treating Jimmy like a slave. 'Go do this, hand me that.' One day, I even heard him order Jimmy to go get him lunch."

"The good thing," the Change Agent told him, "is that you've noticed this behavior. But now we need to do something about it before it gets worse. There are a number of ways we can address this, but from my experience, you will need to address things quickly. The longer a habit lasts, the harder it is to break—and the more of an impact it makes on your company's culture.

"When there is someone on your team creating problems or issues for you, or the other team members, everyone on the team is going to look to you to see how you're going to address it. If you delay in taking action, or worse, don't take action at all, the other employees will see your lack of action as approval or supporting of the behavior.

"Do you think," the Change Agent asked, "that Jeff and Howard were doing a good enough job before Bill's bad behavior started?"

"From what I can tell, yes. But Tom would be a much better judge of that now. He's been dispatching the work, and he is the first and last contact with our customers."

"Have you had any customer complaints about them?"

"Well... to the best of my knowledge, not yet. But I don't wanna start!"

The Change Agent leaned back and steepled his fingers. "Well, for now, it seems Tom has been able to keep your customers happy. Now, we need to find out what Jeff and Howard are feeling. Do you think it might be time to talk to each of them and find out what they see happening? Maybe they can tell you what they're seeing?"

Mark fidgeted. As much as he put forth a tough guy image, Mark actually hated confrontation. He wondered how he would handle it if the new guys told him something he didn't want to hear.

Seeing his discomfort, the Change Agent asked, "What's the worst that could happen?"

Mark thought about it for a moment and said, "They will confirm what I know in my gut... that Bill is making it uncomfortable for them to be here. And I could, potentially, lose them as employees."

"So," the Change Agent suggested, "why don't you spend some time talking with Tom, Jeff and Howard to get their perspective? Let your employees know that you trust them to do a good job and want to do whatever you can to make sure they are happy and productive. See if they bring up anything about Bill. After all—the situation won't simply go away if you ignore it. Although your employees might."

Mark nodded ruefully.

"After you've had time to learn more about what they're feeling, we'll come up with a plan to work through the issues with Bill. Let me know after you've talked with them.

"And in the meantime," the Change Agent said, standing with sweeping grace, "you had some work to do from the last time we met."

Mark turned back and looked up with a slight smirk. He felt pretty good about how he'd done on this homework.

"First," the Change Agent requested, "show me your 90-day SMART goals and your 12-month and 36-month plans."

Mark complied. His list read:

90-day SMART goals plan

1. Document what each employee is doing for the business in the next 30 days. Have them submit it in writing.

2. Onboard and train the two mechanics and have Tom integrate them into the production schedule in the next 60 days.

3. Make it home for dinner once a week starting NOW!

4. Work out three times each week with trainer.

Mark said, "I've struggled with the one-year and three-year plan, because they are basically the same. It may change later, but this is the list I have for now." He showed the Change Agent the list.

Business

- Continue to increase revenue growth.

- Reduce my work hours to 30 hours per week.

- Delegate all tasks that an employee can do, instead of doing them myself.

- Check to make sure new employees are bringing in more revenue than they are costing in compensation.

Personal Goals

- Take a two-week vacation with Kelly and the boys.

- Increase workout schedule to daily.

- Only have employees that I enjoy working with.

Most of these goals still felt impossible to him—but every week, they seemed to get a little closer.

"That's a good list," said the Change Agent. "And a great place for us to start. Planning your future will get easier as time passes. Now, I want you to sit and think about the values and culture of your business.

"What are those things that you hold in highest regard and expect everyone that works for you, and with you, to know and understand?

"Another way to look at this is, if you were to ask your employees, customers, vendors and suppliers what they can expect from you and the business, what would those things be?"

Mark thought about that.

"This list," the Change Agent explained, "will be very important in helping to deal with Bill and the rest of your team. It gives you a written statement of your company's culture. You can use this to tell your employees what you expect from them — and what they can expect from you in return. Does that make sense?"

"I think so," Mark said slowly. It all sounded a little 'fluffy bunny' to him, but his own approach to the problem certainly hadn't been helping.

The Change Agent smiled. "Well, do your best — I'm sure you will get great results!" The Change Agent was pulling something out of his jacket pocket. Mark wondered what it could possibly be this time.

"One last thing," the Change Agent said, handing the velvet bag to Mark. Within the velvet bag was an elegant pewter and wood pen.

The Change Agent continued, "If you ever need to speak with me, just use this pen to write the issue down on a sheet of paper, and I will be there."

Mark responded humbly, "Thank you. It's beautiful."

CHAPTER 6

In the days to come, Mark made sure to block time in his daily schedule to work on the tasks the Change Agent had set before him. His keeping a personal calendar continued to pay off.

After his morning workout, Mark made the time to speak with Tom, Jeff and Howard. Truthfully, he dreaded the conversations and was avoiding the subject, but he kept hearing the Change Agent's words: *"If you delay in taking action, employees will see your reaction as approval."*

Mark knew the conversations were important—and better to get them over with than let the expectation build in his mind.

The truth was hard to hear—yes, Tom, Jeff, and Howard felt like Bill was making it difficult for them to do their jobs. They said sometimes he 'corrected' them even when they knew that they were doing something right, and his micromanaging actually made it hard to get things done.

They seemed relieved that Mark was talking to them about this—and Mark realized that the Change Agent had been exactly right. Because Mark hadn't spoken *against* Bill's actions, Tom, Jeff, and Howard had just assumed that Mark was the same way, and that Bill's attitude was the culture of the business. It was a wonder, he thought, that none of them had left yet!

As Howard left his office — the last of the stressful morning conversations — Mark set his jaw. Bill didn't get to decide the culture of Mark's business.

Mark would have to figure out what to do with Bill, and soon.

Just after lunch, Mark scheduled time to work on his values and the business culture.

He had first viewed this as a chore, an arduous solving of a problem he wished he didn't have. But as he got to work, he found himself unexpectedly excited about the assignment. Envisioning what his ideal business would look like was fun!

He pictured a future where all of his employees were jovial. Glad to be there, glad to see their customers. He pictured a future where they did great work because they *wanted* to — not because he, or Bill, was breathing down their necks. That would be a business he could be proud of.

When at last his notes were completed to his satisfaction, he realized he needed to talk to the Change Agent. So he took out the special pen the Change Agent had given him at their last meeting and wrote the following on a piece of paper…

Can we meet at breakfast to talk about Bill?

#

"Ah, yes!" the Change Agent exclaimed brightly, tucking his napkin into the neck of his tailored suit like a bib. "Thank you for the invitation to breakfast. It is always wonderful to see a good friend. The last time we met, you had two challenges: your problem with Bill and possibly the other mechanics, and the question of your company culture and how you'd define it."

The Change Agent looked at Mark expectantly, waiting for him to choose a course.

Mark thought about the conversations he'd had with Tom, Jeff and Howard yesterday. "I think I need some guidance with how I deal with Bill," he blurted. "All the conversations were the same... Bill was bossy, pushy, and doesn't seem to want to get the work done."

"Yes," the Change Agent acknowledged. "You have had some trouble with Bill in the past, haven't you?"

Mark nodded ruefully.

"Well, you see, that might be because you and Scott did not *intentionally* establish a culture when you started this company."

Mark looked at the Change Agent blankly.

"Mark," the Change Agent explained, "if the owner of a business doesn't set the vision and culture for a business, the employees will. And in my experience, the owners will not like the result."

Mark nodded.

"You and Scott started the business with a vision in mind, but never bothered to put it into words. You didn't consider that, someday, you'd have to share that vision with your employees, so they would understand."

"How do you know we didn't do that?" Mark challenged weakly. He was curious about just how *much* the Change Agent knew about his history.

"Because," the Agent said simply, "if you had been building culture from day one, the problems you've experienced with Bill in the past wouldn't have happened, and your business would have grown much faster than it has."

Mark leaned forward, intrigued. Maybe there was a *reason* all those Silicon Valley guys who talked about 'corporate culture' were rich, after all.

"For your employees to do what you want, they must first *know* what you want," the Change Agent explained. "I know that sounds obvious, but perhaps it is not. To you, your business is a vision that you create. To you, it may be obvious that things *should* be one way and not another. To your employees, it may simply be a to-do list that they must get done. They may not have thought of all the things that need to happen to make it great. Indeed, you are the delegator of tasks—it is arguably not their job to do so!"

"That is sort of how Bill treats it," Mark admitted. "He always has."

"Correct." The Change Agent wagged his finger. "So to fix that, we must share your vision of the company with all your current employees and the new people that may become employees in the future. That way, they will know exactly what you want them to create for you. Does that sound doable?"

"Sure," Mark agreed. "I took some notes after our last meeting."

Mark pulled out the paper with his culture notes on them. The Change Agent looked them over approvingly. "Very good, very good," the Change Agent said. "How would I *know* your employees were doing what you've asked? What could I measure, or at least observe, to say that this goal had been reached?"

"Well," Mark pondered, "I want to have the highest levels of customer service of anybody around. I want my customers to know they're taken care of when they come to my business."

The Change Agent nodded. "'The highest levels of customer service.' Write that down."

By the time breakfast was over, they had written down Mark's vision:

5. The Highest Levels of Customer Service to our internal and external customers

6. The Timely delivery of High-Quality products or services in all we do

7. Open and Honest communication to all concerned, so there are no surprises

8. Teamwork to make things happen quickly and efficiently

The Change Agent nodded approvingly — seemingly both at Mark and at his eggs Benedict.

"Very good. Now that you have this written down, how can you share it with your employees, so they can help make it a reality?"

Mark looked thoughtful. "I can write these down on papers and pass them out — or I can put them on the walls of the shop, so everyone can see! I've seen that in the offices of some of my bigger customers. Then, I guess, there's no room for Bill to argue with anyone about what they're supposed to be doing."

The Change agent kept nodding. "That's a start. We'll talk about some other ways you can use this valuable information in the future — in hiring, customer relations, and more! Let me know how the culture meeting goes," said the Change Agent as he shook Mark's hand and turned toward the door.

Mark nodded enthusiastically. Why hadn't he thought of this before?

By the time he was ready to head into the shop, Mark's head was so full of ideas for his company culture that he wasn't thinking of anything else!

#

Before the shop opened the next day, Mark called everyone into the lunchroom for his 'culture meeting.' He still felt funny thinking about culture — when he was growing up, that was a fancy word that didn't have anything to do with cars. But the Change Agent was right — what he had been doing so far *hadn't* been working, so what was the worst that could happen?

At the Change Agent's suggestion, Mark had brought a nice bagel tray and a box of donuts to the meeting. "If you wish to create a culture of giving," the Change Agent had suggested, "you must lead by example, by giving to your employees."

Amy looked a little too delighted with this new development, and Jimmy was piling a plate high with donuts. Tom, Jeff and Howard sat around the table with their coffee and Jeff grabbed a bagel. Bill sat in his chair at the opposite end of the table from Mark, looking suspicious.

When the team had settled down, Mark cleared his throat. "Ahem. I've brought you all here today to talk about—our company culture."

Amy clapped her hands together. "Ooh! Do we have a mission statement now?"

Mark grinned. "No, but thanks for being so excited. We'll create our mission statement together at a later meeting. For now, it's important to me that you understand my vision and culture for this business. We're just now putting into words the way I've felt for a long time. Our vision and culture are summed up in these few sentences I call our Commitment Statement."

Mark handed out a paper to each member of his team. Printed on the papers were the words:

We Commit to...

- The Highest Levels of Customer Service to our internal and external customers

- The Timely delivery of High-Quality products or services in all we do

- Open and Honest communication with everyone concerned, so there are no surprises

- Teamwork to make everything happen quickly and efficiently

Mark looked around the room. "We've hired Jeff and Howard to help ease our workload, and to make sure our customers experience everything on our Commitment Statement. That's how we build our reputation—and that's how we grow."

Mark continued, "Jeff, Howard, we're happy to have you here. If you need anything, please let me, Tom or Amy know. We're the best auto shop out there—and everybody's gonna know it!

"I know this may seem a little formal and different from the way things have been in the past. I realized that if we all want a better workplace—this is how we do it. I will find time to meet with each one of you individually in the next week to discuss your thoughts about these changes."

Tom, Jimmy, Jeff, Howard and Amy actually applauded.

Bill just sat there with a look of frustration on his face.

CHAPTER 7

In the next week, Tom started a daily 'morning huddle' meeting before they opened the doors to customers. These were short, fifteen-minute meetings where everyone met out on the shop floor. They reviewed the day's schedule, shared any issues or challenges they were anticipating, and everyone had the opportunity to understand the role they played in taking care of their customers. Everyone seemed to enjoy and appreciate the meetings—except possibly Bill.

After the group broke up from their morning meeting, Amy approached Mark nervously. "I need to talk to you," she said, "about Bill."

"Oh, yeah?" Mark braced himself.

"I'm worried. Bill is doing basically nothing to help out. He's been training Jimmy, but his idea of training the kid seems to be eating a sandwich while he watches him work. Bill makes conversation with anyone who will listen. Jimmy told me Bill complained to *him* about Tom trying to get him to work last week. Mark... I don't think he wants to be here."

Mark pinched the bridge of his nose. For the first time in a few weeks, his headache was back. "Okay. Thanks for telling me, Amy. I'll talk to him."

But instead of going straight to Bill, Mark went into his office and used his special pen to write these words...

Can we meet?

The knock came on his office door before he could put the pen on the desk.

Mark opened the door to see the Change Agent peering at him.

Mark started. "I, ah. I need some help."

The Change Agent entered as silently as a wraith, and Mark tried to get that image out of his head.

"Bill?" the Change Agent guessed.

"Yeah. Amy confirmed my suspicions that he's just not doing much when I'm not around. And, given her comments, it seems like everyone is seeing it. What do I do?"

The Change Agent steepled his fingers solemnly. "Well, it does sound like you have quite a quandary on your hands. Sometimes when a team member doesn't want to fill his job description, there's not much that can be done. But there is one last, important and effective technique that you could try."

Mark listened anxiously.

"One option for you," the Change Agent said, "is to give Bill the option of being a productive member of the team by adhering to the Commitment Statement that you've presented. Or," he continued, "the other option is that he 'deselects' himself from being part of the company's culture. He doesn't *have* to work here, you know."

Mark winced.

The Change Agent continued, "You've acknowledged that the defined vision and culture is new, and much different from when you and Bill first started working together. And, it's what you need to grow your business and take back your own life. Now that you've taken the time to create your Commitment Statement and put it down on paper, you need to ask Bill a simple question, and get a simple answer: 'Do you want to be part of what we're building here?'"

Mark bit his lip.

"Let Bill know that if he chooses *yes*, then you will expect his one hundred percent commitment and follow-through on all responsibilities assigned and all direction he is given—whether you're here, or not.

"But if Bill chooses *no*, then he is deselecting himself from being employed here. It does not mean he's a bad employee or that you're a bad boss. It just means that the relationship is not the right fit any longer. No hard feelings."

Mark was busily jotting down notes as the Change Agent spoke. He couldn't remember the last time he'd felt like he was learning so much.

The Change Agent paused and crossed his legs, folding his hands on his knee. "This will be a difficult conversation, Mark. Do you have any questions about how to approach it?"

Mark looked up and sighed. "No, but part of me wishes you could go and have this conversation with him for me. The other part knows it's something I need to do myself."

The Change Agent nodded. "It is essential to your growth as a business owner, and as the leader of a team." Then he smiled. "Mark, I know you can do this. Go forth, and coach Bill to help him identify what he wants!"

#

Mark and Bill moved back to the empty lunchroom for some privacy. Bill seemed to know what was coming.

Mark said, "Bill, thanks for agreeing to meet with me. I wanted to talk about the Commitment Statement."

Bill nodded and scratched his chin. "Fancy words, but how's this different from what we've been doing?"

"Well, Bill," Mark said honestly, "that's just it. Sometimes I feel like when I leave the shop—there's no guarantee that your work is gonna get done. I don't know why that is, but—if we're *all* going to do well, everyone needs to step up and clearly understand the rules and expectations."

Mark went on to share the options that had been outlined by the Change Agent. "You can stay here, Bill, and follow directions and work with the team—or you can look for a job somewhere else. If you don't like the changes we're making, I understand."

Bill looked thoughtful. He was surprisingly quiet—and seemed almost relieved? It was as though he knew, too, that a tension that had been building for many years was about to be resolved.

"So, Bill," Mark soldiered on, "do you have any questions? It may not be easy, but the decision is completely yours to make. This is important. Take a few days to think things over and figure out what's best for you. I'll put you in my calendar for ten a.m. on Friday. We'll sit down together so you can tell me your decision."

#

Bill arrived at the shop on Friday, just before ten a.m., and went straight for Mark's office. Mark knew by looking at Bill's face what he had decided.

"Bill," he said. "Thanks for being on time. Have you made a decision about what you want to do?"

Bill nodded slowly. "I've thought a lot about what you said. The shop is a lot different now than the way it was when you, Scott and I were doing the work. These changes may be better for the business, but not better for me. With the other mechanics, you don't need me anymore.

"I appreciate the opportunity to be part of this, but I don't like all the changes. I talked it over with my wife, and we're just going to go away for a few weeks and decide what we're going to do. If it's okay with you, I'm going to go and say goodbye to everyone now. I will be back later today with my truck to pick up my tools and drop off my keys."

CHAPTER 8

As the days passed, Mark found that it was true what the Change Agent had said about time passing slowly when you're making changes. As he began to make more changes around the shop and re-evaluate his goals frequently, two weeks felt like an eternity!

Mark's confidence in making changes was increasing, and at times he felt like he could do anything! But there were also times when he wasn't quite sure what *to* do.

He was still a little bit afraid of trying new things, and half-expecting something to go wrong with the changes he'd already made.

Mark was developing a habit: Each morning after he got back from going for a walk or going to see his trainer, he had his coffee and sat at his desk, asking himself, "How am I going to invest my time today? Do these things move me toward my longer-term plans?"

He found as he made his way through the day that if he took the time to block space in his calendar, more things seemed to get done, whether it was helping Amy come up with a more efficient system for ordering, working with Tom to make sure customers were cared for, checking with Jeff and Howard to make sure they had all they needed, talking with Jimmy and showing him a few new tricks, or calling a videographer to talk about filming some customer testimonials — an idea that had struck him during one of his morning coffee breaks.

There were still bumps in the road as Mark tried to stay on his schedule. Some projects required a few hours and a great deal of Mark's focus, but Mark kept getting interrupted by phone calls, emails, and Amy coming into Mark's office to bother him with the littlest things.

So, one day when a knock came on his office door, Mark was certain it was her. He looked up, ready to object — but instead, it was the Change Agent who slipped into his office and closed the door quietly behind him.

"How do you — *why* do you — you know what, never mind!" Mark took a deep breath, feeling his heart rate slow.

The Change Agent sat down in what was becoming his usual seat. "So," he inquired, eyebrows raised, "how are things going?"

Mark breathed deeply. "Well," he began, "Bill decided to deselect himself from the shop. That went much better than I had expected, to be honest. He left on good terms and the rest of the team seems much happier, now that he has been gone a few weeks."

Mark ticked off the matters he could think of on his fingers. "Using the calendar is working great, but I've struggled with knowing *what* to do. The other thing that's really sticking out now that I have scheduled my days are the distractions. Things that keep me from what I should be working on, and I don't know how to make them stop."

The Change Agent nodded sagely. "It is amazing," he commented, "how much time you realize you've been wasting, once you have your time in order.

"A good piece of advice for any situation is this: When you feel like you may be losing direction and focus, go back to your goals and plans. If you are serving those, you will never go astray. If you're not... well..." The Change Agent cleared his throat politely and gave Mark a meaningful glance.

"At the end of each quarter, you should revisit your SMART goals and determine

1. What was accomplished

2. What is in progress

3. What still needs to be done

"When you're doing that review, you measure those SMART Goals against your longer-term plans to make sure they are still valid. Sometimes, you learn something along the way that makes you realize that what you first thought you wanted actually is not the best way to proceed.

"Then, re-write your 90-day SMART goals and put them in priority: Which things, when completed, will have the biggest impact on the business?

"You've met an important SMART goal—you've hired two mechanics. Although you were stressed at the thought of doing that, the fact is that all the positive changes you've been able to make were enabled by the addition of Jeff and Howard."

Mark nodded. He had become acutely aware of that himself.

"Now," the Change Agent continued, "let's talk about the distractions you've mentioned.

"Distractions will eat your time, because they force you to move your time and attention off a project and onto them. You have one hundred percent control over your time-eaters and how you choose to deal with them.

"If you don't want phone calls, then turn your phone off. If you don't want to hear the notification that you have mail, then turn it off. If people keep interrupting you, closing your door may help.

"Now, about being interrupted by employees as a business owner, that's a little more delicate. You should explain that if there is an emergency – the potential loss of life, health or great deal of money – then you want to be interrupted.

"But, if the thing they want to talk to you about can wait, then have them write it down on paper, so ideas and concerns won't be forgotten. Then you can set a regular and exclusive appointment with them to go over those things they think you should know.

"While a lot of people are frustrated with the way they are managing time, everyone's specific issues are different. Buried under the chaos of confusion are clues of individual strengths and weaknesses as well as personality style and preferences: your unique sources of energy and what makes you happy.

"So, we need to begin the process of custom-designing a solution that will be a true match for who you are. Your relationship with time has three parts:

1. What Works

By listing what *is* working in your schedule and your time management routine, your confidence will receive a boost and you will discover the time management skills you have created. This will give you a clue of what appeals to you and give you information to fix the areas that are not working.

If you find time to clean your car, for example, then that means you may find a purely physical task therapeutic. If you're mainly involved in mental work, then thirty minutes a day on physical exercise — non-mental — may be enough to recharge you and heighten your energy.

2. What's Not Working

Your answers to this question become your list of everything you want to fix. Compare your list of 'what's not working' to your list of 'what *is* working.'

If you are having trouble starting and finishing things, then you may be able to isolate the reason why. In some cases, you may just need to develop certain skills or apply a skill from one area of your life to another.

You may have no problem delegating at work, so you might simply apply the same system at home.

3. Your Energy Cycles and Sources

In some cases, we may struggle with some tasks more than others not because of our skill level, but because of individual preferences.

Tuning into these natural inclinations can help explain why certain items are landing on your *what's not working* and *what is working* lists. If you thrive on a fast pace, for example, you will know how to fill your day with many activities. If you prefer a slower, more thoughtful rate of work, it might be that task-switching takes a tremendous amount of energy for you, and you'd be most efficient if you consolidated to work on similar tasks in one day.

In addition to your natural preferences, the ups and downs of your energy can have a profound effect on your to-do list.

Energy is power; it enables you to work toward your goals. Once you understand your energy sources and cycles, you can begin to manage them. Since you can't always control when you do certain tasks, the best time to be tuned into what activities fuel your energy is when it is flagging.

Sometimes a change of pace is all you need to boost your energy levels. If you have been concentrating for hours and your brain needs a break, it's a great time to do a task that requires movement and using your muscles."

The Change Agent smiled. "You are fortunate, Mark, in that your work naturally involves both mental and physical tasks. I often counsel business owners who sit at desks all day to go for walks throughout the day to keep their brains and bodies humming. You can do that; but you can also exercise right here."

Mark was nodding thoughtfully to himself. He *had* noticed that sometimes, if he sat around his home office for too long, he'd eventually find himself pacing around the house. He'd been chiding himself for 'losing focus' during those moments, but perhaps the Change Agent was right. Perhaps his body was just regulating its energy levels.

"Thank you again. I—"

But by the time Mark looked up to finish his heartfelt thank you, the Change Agent was gone.

CHAPTER 9

Mark reclined on a lawn chair next to Kelly. The sun was setting, sending orange and pink and crimson through the trees. In the yard in front of them, Ethan and Jacob were kicking a soccer ball back and forth.

He'd bought these chairs after realizing how beautiful the sunset was from their own backyard — now that he got out of work early enough to see it. He didn't *need* plane tickets to take a family vacation, it turned out — but he'd bought them anyway. Next month, he and Kelly and the boys were going to Aruba.

It had been a little over a year since the Change Agent came into their lives. Mark had asked Kelly where she found him, and she only looked at him in confusion. "I thought *you* found him," she said.

They'd both come to understand that their new friend was a little bit special — one of those things that's too special to question. And the rewards of his intervention had been astounding.

Mark was now working thirty-hour weeks. Tom, Amy, Jimmy and the new mechanics, Jeff and Howard, had everything under control at the shop. Old customers said they missed seeing

Mark around, but they appreciated the fresh and friendly new faces. The shop was projected to add another strong increase in revenue this year — even more than in past years.

Mark's health was improving. When he'd started, he thought walking three times a week would be impossible. But now, his trainer had him working out five days a week. Mark hadn't had a headache in months and had lost fifteen pounds in the process of getting fit.

The hardest part of Mark's journey was learning to trust his employees. After building his reputation — and his prosperity — on the work of his own hands, it was difficult for him to imagine anyone else being able to keep his customers.

But Mark's customers had stuck with his business — and with Tom at the helm, they were as happy as ever.

Mark was now free to enjoy his life. He still worked at the shop, greeting customers and managing relationships with vendors. But most of the routine work he *had been* doing was now being taken care of by others, who were all the happier for feeling like they had what they needed to be great at their jobs.

As the sun sank below the horizon, the first evening stars began to come out. One of them blazed bright and clear above the tree line.

"Kids," Kelly called, rising from her lawn chair, "time to come in! You've got school in the morning!"

As she shepherded the faintly protesting boys into the house, Mark sat for a moment longer, looking up at the budding stars.

"Hello, Mark," said a familiar voice behind him.

Mark turned to see the Change Agent standing a respectful distance from his chair. The Change Agent was looking up at the same star he was.

"Hey!" Mark rose from his chair and extended his hand to the Agent. The Change Agent took it and shook it, firmly. There was something final about the gesture.

"I now see that you have everything you need to reach your goals," the Change Agent said softly. "You have learned very well. Congratulations!"

"All thanks to you," Mark said, and was surprised to feel himself tearing up.

"If you should ever have need of me in the future," the Change Agent said firmly, "you have your pen. Just write your question or concern on a piece of paper. I will come."

"I—*why? Why* are you doing all this?" was all Mark could think to ask.

"To pay it forward." The Change Agent winked.

And he was gone.

JOAN AND THE TROUBLED TEAM

CHAPTER 1

It was ten a.m. on a Saturday when Joan's phone rang.

She picked it up and felt sick when she saw that it was the salon's number calling. She thought for a long moment about not answering. Finally, with a sigh, she pulled her car over — so much for a relaxing day off — and swiped to answer.

"Hello?"

"Hi! Joan? I'm so glad you answered. Ramone isn't here."

Joan closed her eyes. She wished she could say she was surprised. This was the third time this year that one of her employees simply hadn't shown up for their shift.

Which would be less of a problem if this were the kind of work that another employee could cover for.

"What about Jacquelyn?"

"She's already here, and she's fully booked for the day. So am I. Theresa's in North Carolina with her mom. We could *try* to handle Ramone's appointments between the three of us here, but the first one is already waiting and she's asking what's taking so long."

Joan bit her tongue. "I'm coming in."

The relief on the other end of the line was audible. "Oh, thank you, Joan. I knew you'd want to know."

Yes. Joan did want to know when her employees didn't show up — because often, her covering for them herself was the only way to solve it. She didn't know how she was supposed to grow her business this way, let alone enjoy the leisure that was supposed to come with being a business owner. But she also didn't know what she was supposed to do about it.

Joan pulled back out into traffic and turned the car around to head toward the salon.

She'd never realized when she worked for her first boss, Sarah, what a nightmare being a business owner was. She came to work every day, made her clients look fabulous, and collected her fees. She had always had the impression that Sarah had it pretty good — as a business owner, all she had to do was provide the equipment and facilities, right?

But now Joan understood why Sarah decided not to rebuild after the fire that burned her salon down. Owning a business, in Joan's experience, was a nightmare.

At first, it had seemed only logical that Joan should buy a building and provide a place for her fellow stylists to work. Joan and her husband talked it over, and they agreed they would invest their retirement savings into the project to create an environment that she knew her clients would love. After all—she'd been booked up whenever she chose to work under Sarah, and her station had been decorated with the thank you notes and birthday cards her clients sent her!

But after she bought the building, the right furniture and expensive equipment, Joan didn't just want her stylists to come and go as they pleased, the way she had as an independent contractor under Sarah. She wanted the scheduling, marketing and all the payments to go through her. How else was she going to make sure she could pay back her investment?

She had quickly discovered just how hard it was to be the owner of a salon.

First, her equipment and inventory started to go missing. She never determined who was taking it, but two of the stylists she'd hired had quit within six months. One of them simply said she "had to get something from her car" and never came back.

So, she started grilling her prospective new employees about their employment history before hiring them—anyone who had worked a previous job for less than six months was out. But it didn't seem to be helping. She'd lost two more employees in the last year.

Joan doubted she would see Ramone again. Ramone knew that Joan had a zero-tolerance policy for employees missing shifts. If he wasn't here today, he likely wouldn't be back.

Which would be less of a problem if she could find a way to make sure Ramone's customers could be taken care of. Joan's employees usually booked appointments as far as a month in advance.

Joan's clients loved Joan's work. But the last-minute substitutions and occasional poor-quality work of her other employees had led to her company getting mixed reviews on Yelp, with some customers saying, "it seems like the owner doesn't care."

These comments made Joan's blood boil. Of *course*, she cared. Why didn't her employees?

Joan pulled into the parking lot and looked up at her business. From the outside, it looked amazing. But she couldn't help feeling stressed when she looked at her storefront now. So many things had gone wrong that she was beginning to hate this business.

Joan took a deep breath, put on her best customer service smile, and walked inside.

CHAPTER 2

Despite her concerns over the business, Joan was feeling pretty good when she finished what was supposed to be Ramone's shift. The customers were surprised to see her, but pleasantly so. When they asked where Ramone was, she told them Ramone was sick—and they gushed about what a good boss she was for covering for her employee.

Joan had always loved working with customers. That was why she rented a chair from Sarah for ten years, and why she decided to open her own salon. She wanted to make sure she always had a place to do what she loved.

If only salon ownership hadn't turned out to be so much more than she'd bargained for.

Joan hummed as she closed up the shop—she had successfully pushed thoughts of the stacks of paperwork and hiring a new stylist out of her mind. For now, she was just riding the high of working with customers all day.

So she was surprised when she turned around and found a slender man in an impeccably-tailored suit standing a few feet away.

He didn't seem to be just a passerby—he looked for all the world like he'd been waiting for her respectfully.

"I'm sorry, sir," Joan said, mustering her best warm smile. "But we're closed for the day." She pulled out a business card. "If you'd like to make an appointment, we'd be happy to schedule you in tomorrow. "

The strange man took Joan's card and inspected it closely. "A fine operation you have here—yes, a fine business indeed," he pronounced. "But I understand you lost a stylist today."

Joan frowned, instantly on guard. Who told him this? Was he a friend of Ramone's?

The man offered a card of his own with a flourish and a slight bow. "I," he said, "am known as the Change Agent. I help business owners like yourself transform their businesses so they can live the lives they want."

Joan stared at him skeptically. Was this really happening? She looked around her empty parking lot. His marketing tactics seemed inefficient, at best.

"My results are guaranteed," the Agent explained, "provided you have two prerequisites."

Joan folded her arms. "And what would those be?"

"Would you say, Joan," the Change Agent asked, "that you have a desire to grow your business?"

Joan thought about it. What she *really* wanted was to be free to cut hair again—but if she could build a team that actually worked, and even expand her business's size, she could quickly pay off the money she'd put into starting the business.

"Yes, I suppose you could say that," Joan said.

"Good," the Change Agent said brightly. "Now, this is the hard part—the one that prevents many business owners from realizing their dream: Are you willing to change the way you do things?"

Joan bristled a little. "Are you suggesting that this is somehow *my* fault?" She'd forgotten about the question of how the Change Agent knew about her problem—it didn't seem to matter. Maybe he'd been reading her Yelp reviews.

"I am suggesting," the Change Agent said smoothly, "that your behavior is the one variable you *can* control—and quite easily at that. Wouldn't it be wonderful if all your problems could be solved by changing the one thing that is entirely within your control?"

Joan admitted that that would be pretty wonderful. "Yes, then... I guess I am open to making some changes."

"Excellent!" the Change Agent beamed. "Now that you have met both of my prerequisites, we can start whenever you're ready!"

It was getting dark. This hardly seemed like the place for a business meeting. "Start what?" she asked suspiciously.

"Why, start transforming your business into what you've always dreamt it to be! All we really need to do that is you."

Joan waited.

"Can you tell me, Miss Joan, what a 'team' is?"

"It's a group of people who work together," Joan responded automatically.

The Change Agent nodded approvingly. "That is true. But is that *all* a team is? Is that the complete definition? Would you call, for example, a group of people who happen to work in the same space, a team?"

"I... no, I guess not." Joan thought about this for a moment. She thought about sports teams, and what motivated them to do their best. Then, she decided, "A team is a group of people who work together *toward a common goal.*"

"Yes!" The Change Agent fell into step beside Joan as she started toward her car. "Now what would you say your team's common goal is?"

That stopped Joan in her tracks. "I... I'm not sure." She thought for several long moments. "I mean, it's better for all of us if our business has a good reputation. I guess that's our common goal."

The Change Agent raised his eyebrows. "But," he asked politely, "is that enough? Your employees don't seem to be having much trouble finding other jobs. Perhaps your offer of a good reputation is not enough to be a good motivator."

Joan had to admit that she needed to think about that.

The Change Agent paused as Joan got out her car keys. It was at that point that she realized there were no other cars in the parking lot. Where had he come from?

"If I may, I'd like to share a universal truth," the Change Agent said. "A business is a direct reflection of its owner. Business owners often hire people who are quite similar to themselves."

Joan felt herself bristling again.

"With that in mind, I'd like you to seriously think about this question. If you were an employee instead of the salon owner, what would motivate *you*?"

Joan frowned as the Change Agent asked that single question. She thought she already had an idea of what the answer was—and she wasn't sure she liked it.

"Thank you," Joan said thoughtfully, "for your insights. You've given me a lot to think about. What do you charge?"

The Change Agent waved his hand, looking aghast. "Oh, there's no charge, dear lady. I do this to pay it forward for other business owners."

"Sure," Joan said, looking at him sidelong. "Sure."

"We shall meet again," he assured her, bowing as she unlocked her car.

Joan paused and looked around the darkened parking lot again. "Do you... need a ride?" She probably shouldn't offer that to a strange man, but he *seemed* harmless.

The Agent dipped his head politely. "Thank you, but I'm quite well taken care of. Enjoy your evening!"

Joan got into her car and realized, after she had shut her car door, that the Change Agent was gone.

CHAPTER 3

Joan had to admit some hard truths to herself over the coming week. She realized that she had been so concerned about making sure she profited from her business, she had lost sight of why she had become a stylist herself to begin with.

Back when she had worked as an independent contractor for Sarah, Joan had loved having the ability to make her own hours, even though it meant she had to find her own clients and buy her own supplies. She had loved the independence of being able to run her business her way and feeling personally responsible for making sure her clients got great results.

As a salon owner, she had wanted her staff to be employees, not independent contractors, so that she could manage all aspects of her business—controlling marketing, quality, cash and customer relationships.

But in the process, she'd taken away the very things that had motivated her to spend seventeen years working as a stylist—the sense of independence, and of personal responsibility for great results.

Joan fretted over what to do about this. If she wanted self-motivated employees, would she have to allow them to make their own hours, too? Would she have to give up some of her control over her business?

She was thinking about this on one of her morning walks when suddenly, someone fell into step beside her.

"Good morning, Joan," greeted the Change Agent. In place of his suit, he now wore a bright purple jumpsuit—something that looked like it came directly out of the nineteen-eighties!

"Hello," Joan acknowledged. Right now, she didn't care what he was wearing. "Is now a... good time for us to talk?"

"That's why I'm here," the Change Agent said with a nod of his head.

Joan slowed her pace a little. "I invested a great deal of thought on what you said. And I came to some troubling conclusions."

"Do tell," the Change Agent encouraged her.

"If my employees are like me, I'll have to give them more independence to motivate them to stay. But I'm afraid to do that. What if no one wants to work evenings or weekends? Those are our busiest hours!"

The Change Agent nodded sagely. "It's true that your employees might feel motivated if they had more independence. But that is only part of what they want. What else?"

"Well," Joan explained, "when I was an independent, I liked the sense of accomplishment I got. I didn't mind having to buy my own supplies and find my own clients, as long as I felt good about what I did for them and they were happy."

The Change Agent nodded approvingly. "Very good. That sounds like the beginning of a good corporate culture."

Joan slowed her pace, deep in thought. "Corporate culture? Isn't that something that those tech companies do?"

"Corporate culture," the Change Agent explained, "is something *every* business has. Every group, organization or business develops a culture — that just means a set of shared values and understandings about how things are done.

"The only question is," the Change Agent peered at Joan, "are you creating your business's culture, or are you letting your employees do it for you?"

Joan thought about that. Often, her employees did not seem on the same page as her. Many of them had frustrating habits, such as complaining about their schedules — even to their customers. Some of her employees refused to clean up after themselves at their stations and in the breakroom, which created a feeling of disarray and apathy. Those negative things almost seemed contagious to other employees, and even to her Yelp reviews!

Complaining, disarray and apathy — was that the culture of Joan's business?

"I guess I'm not creating the culture," Joan admitted. "But... how do you create one? I've never heard anybody talk about doing that before."

The Change Agent sat down on a bench beside the jogging trail, and Joan followed suit.

"As the great business leader, Ram Charan said, 'The culture of an organization is simply the collective behavior of its leaders.' If the business leader is not engaged enough with their employees to set an example — then employees will follow *each other's* examples. When there's no good example in the mix, bad behaviors spread.

"Leaders who are out of touch with their employees often cause low productivity, dwindling morale, high employee turnover, and low employee engagement. If the employee feels that their boss treats them like a piece of equipment to be measured and replaced if necessary, they are much less motivated to work.

"On the other hand, employees who feel a connection to their leader are often highly productive and engaged in their work. Having a greater understanding of the dynamics of their working relationship will help all parties appreciate where their perspectives are similar, and where they differ.

"It might sound strange," the Change Agent said, "but this mutual understanding will result in a more productive and positive working relationship."

That would certainly explain a lot. Joan thought harder.

"I *thought* I was engaged with my employees," she said finally. "I spend a lot of time at the salon. I spend a lot of time on the phone with my employees, too."

"What do you do when you're at the salon?" the Change Agent asked.

"Well, I'm usually working with customers. Or I'm in the office, handling expenses. Or I..." Joan felt a little sheepish admitting this, though she wasn't sure why. "... am telling my employees what to do."

"Mm. So your employees don't see you much, do they? Except when you're telling them what to do."

"I guess that's true."

"Maybe that's what they take away from your example, then. That people in your business need to be told what to do, or they simply expect other people to do things."

Joan winced.

"Being a leader," the Change Agent said sympathetically, "is much harder than most people think. When leaders aren't invested in their business and their employees, then employees aren't invested in their leader or their business.

"Leaders have to *demonstrate* the values they want their employees to have. Simply telling people what to do—well, that gives employees the impression that that's how they should behave, too."

"That sounds like it could take a lot of my time," Joan said, concerned.

"How much time are you already spending dealing with crises, or finding new employees?"

"That's a good point," Joan admitted.

The Change Agent steepled his fingers. "A leader," he reflected, "is different from a manager. A manager simply prevents things from going wrong; a leader makes things happen and creates new possibilities. Or, as another great leader, Admiral Grace Hopper, liked to say, 'You manage things; you lead people.'

"If you ask one hundred people to define leadership," the Change Agent continued, "you will likely get at least one hundred different answers. Leadership takes many forms and styles. But most of the one hundred people would agree that without a leader, they would likely fail at what they do!"

Joan was impressed. "It sounds like leaders are pretty important people."

"It is a very valuable skill set," the Change Agent agreed. "And probably the most reliable difference between a successful business and an unsuccessful one.

"Here are the top TEN words used to define a strong leader:

Visionary

Good Communicator

Risk-taker

Integrity

Someone who makes things happen

Influencer

Empowerment

Congruent

Respect

Confidence."

"That's... an intimidating list," Joan said.

"It is," the Change Agent agreed. "But which of those words do you think you are *already* good at?"

"Well, I'm plenty good at taking risks," Joan said, thinking back to her conversations with her husband to convince him to invest their retirement savings to open her business. "And I guess you could say I make things happen," she said, remembering how all of the other stylists who worked in Sarah's salon had talked about starting a business—but only she had done it! "And I like to think I'm confident. I'm not too sure about the rest."

"Well," the Change Agent suggested, "why don't we look at the other items on this list? We'll talk about all of these, but let's start at the top.

"For the next few weeks, ask yourself what your *vision* for your company is. What would your perfect company look like? How would its employees—and its leadership—behave?"

Joan shook her head and laughed. "I'm not sure my 'vision' counts for much."

"Joan," the Change Agent chided, suddenly serious, "everything in the universe is created twice. First in our minds, then in our reality. If you forget the first step, you cannot complete the second!"

Joan sat, a little bit shaken by that. She'd always thought that daydreaming was silly—but the Change Agent was right. How could she create what she wanted, if she didn't imagine it first?

"I will leave you to that task," he said, standing with a polite nod of his head.

As he jogged away, Joan thought that, somehow, he really was pulling off that purple jumpsuit.

CHAPTER 4

For the next few weeks, Joan thought long and hard about what she wanted her business to look like. Her utopia was easy to describe: a business where her customers were raving fans, the employees got the same flexibility and satisfaction she had had as an independent stylist, and she as the business owner also enjoyed huge profits and a great reputation.

It was easy to describe; it was harder for her to imagine how she could make it a reality.

Still, Joan tried. She wrote down her vision for the company, and revisited and tweaked it each night.

She also kept some of the Change Agent's other leadership descriptions in her head. What did it mean to 'engage with employees?' To 'be invested in them?'

What did it mean to show integrity, empowerment, and respect for her employees? How could she be congruent? And, what did it mean to be a good communicator?

Joan thought about this each morning over coffee and read about these skills and values on the internet. It wasn't too long before she found a few opportunities to change some things—and noticed some surprising results.

She made a point of stopping to talk to her employees when she went into the salon. She asked them about their lives and expressed empathy when they complained. That had to count as engagement, right?

After a few weeks of engaging more, she noticed something strange. Was it her imagination, or was the breakroom getting less and less messy with each passing day?

Making a point of talking to her stylists in the morning led to more natural conversation with them throughout the day. Soon, they were going out of their way to make her customers' visits go smoothly. Not because they were afraid of her, she realized: They were treating her like a *teammate*.

This, she thought, was how things had been when she'd worked at Sarah's salon. It was great to be back!

But bumps in the road continued. Two of her stylists didn't respond well to attempts at conversation; Linda seemed almost scared, while Theresa was curt and uninterested. These two seemed to get more anxious and more irritated the harder Joan tried to connect with them.

After a few weeks of opening up to her stylists, her receptionist, Carol, said something to Joan that explained a lot.

"Theresa and Linda," Carol said, "sure do switch shifts a lot. I don't think Theresa has worked a weekend in six months."

That set off alarm bells in Joan's head. Part of the employee agreement was that *every* stylist would work her share of weekend shifts. Theresa should have been working at least one each month.

One by one, she found time to talk to the other stylists privately.

All of them had a similar story to tell: Theresa approached them to ask them to work her weekend shifts. She always had a pressing reason, like a wedding, or a class, or a family emergency. But every weekend she was supposed to work, she came up with something new.

Most of the stylists had eventually stopped responding to Theresa's requests and pointed out that they had all agreed to abide by the schedule when they started working here. But Linda was the newest stylist, fresh out of cosmetology school. She had apparently been agreeing to switch shifts with Theresa. A lot.

Joan frowned. The Change Agent's statements had made her think—had she failed in some way as a leader, to allow this to happen? Her first instinct was to give Theresa a stern talking-to—but there might be a larger problem. And as the Change Agent had said, just telling her employees what to do hadn't been getting the results she wanted.

She wished that she could talk to the Change Agent now...

And just like that, he walked into the salon.

Carol was asking brightly if the Change Agent had an appointment when Joan hurried up to him.

"He's with me," she said, ushering the Change Agent to her office at the back of the salon. She shut the door behind them, relieved to have privacy.

"Joan," the Change Agent greeted her. "How have things been going since we last met?"

"I thought they were going pretty well," Joan said unhappily. "I've been spending a lot of time envisioning my perfect company and engaging with the team, but today..." She told him what had happened.

The Change Agent sat down in the chair across from Joan's desk at her invitation. "Ahh," he said. "That is troubling."

"So, what do I do? Is this my fault?"

"Well," the Change Agent began, "it sounds as though you have already taken some important steps toward creating an environment where this won't happen anymore. But it also sounds like there is more to be done."

"What's that?" Joan asked, anxious to take the next step.

"You said you had made some progress. Why don't you show me your vision statement?"

Joan pulled the wrinkled, folded and re-folded paper out of her pocket. It now read:

To be a company …

- Where employees love what they do and feel a tremendous sense of pride and accomplishment in their work

- Where the employees take care of themselves and each other

- Where customers get stellar service and always come back

- Where all the employees feel nurtured and supported in achieving their personal and professional goals

- Where everyone is happy

The Change Agent read the list over, nodding approvingly. "Very nice," he murmured. "I would very much like to see this company come into existence."

"But *how* do we do it?" Joan lamented. "It seems like I can't keep employees without being on their backs all the time!"

"Or," the Change Agent asked gently, "are your employees leaving *because* you are on their backs all the time?"

Joan was dumbfounded. That had never occurred to her.

"Your vision statement," the Change Agent said, "is important. We need to have everyone gain a clear understanding of your vision for the business. But, what's not to like? They take care of your business, and each other — and you give them a tremendous sense of accomplishment and a workplace where everyone is taken care of."

"But *how*," Joan asked, "do I do that?"

"Have you ever heard," the Change Agent asked, "of a 'team day?' This is a time when your employees are together to learn, exchange and engage as a team. The length of time of a team day is usually three to six hours. But the time together is not as important as the ground rules that apply to everyone there: All opinions are valid and important, there are no hidden agendas, and everyone is expected to provide open and honest communication.

"During your first team day, you should be able to accomplish four things.

1. You can share your vision with your employees and make sure they all understand what that means.

2. Then, we can have them create their Mission Statement."

Joan interrupted, looking puzzled. "Mission Statement?"

"Yes! If your vision for the business is the *what* you want to accomplish, the mission statement is the *how*. Your employees can work through the things they will do to help make sure your vision becomes reality. The big plus is that, when they do this, they will take ownership over the mission because they were part of creating it. It is their mission as much as it is yours."

He continued, "Team days are also useful for:

3.   Having the team create a schedule of future team days and any specific discussion topics they'd like to cover.

4.   Creating a list of SMART goals that will help you make your Mission Statement happen."

"SMART goals?" Joan was starting to feel a little silly repeating things the Change Agent said—but she'd learned long ago that it was more important to ask questions than to look smart.

"Yes!" the Change Agent beamed. "SMART goals can help you and your team to find concrete, measurable steps to reach your goals. If you know exactly what the steps are, and when you must have them completed, it is almost impossible to fail!

"SMART stands for:

Specific -That means you know precisely what steps you must take to accomplish this goal.

Measurable - That means there are metrics and outcomes you can look at that will tell you whether or not this goal has been achieved.

Achievable - This means these are actions you can really take, right now. There are *always* achievable steps you can take toward your goals.

Results-focused - This means that your goals are designed to directly create your desired outcome. And,

Time-bound - This means you give yourself a deadline, so the steps cannot be put off indefinitely.

"Now then," the Change Agent challenged Joan, "we've covered quite a bit. *In the next three months,* what are some of the things you'd like to make happen to make your vision a reality?"

Joan thought hard. She pulled a piece of paper out of her desk drawer and, slowly, thoughtfully, began to write.

1. Effectively share the vision for the salon with all employees

   o Schedule regular team days

   o Have them engage in developing a mission statement

   o Create a list of SMART goals to move us toward realizing the mission and vision

2. Find ways to engage and build relationships with each of the team

   o Learn about each employee's personal and professional goals

- o Give employees a sense of support—privately ask them what they need to accomplish more

- o Give each employee a chance to be on the team or to deselect themselves

3. Make sure employees know exactly what they are responsible for—and what specific things they can do or achieve to be successful

4. Hire new employees who will embrace the vision and culture

The Change Agent looked over Joan's list approvingly. When he got to the bottom, he chuckled. "For now," he said, "let's focus on keeping the employees you already have. It looks like you already have some good ideas about how to do that. We will cover some things you should know before hiring new team members soon!"

Joan took the list back from the Change Agent and looked at him attentively, her pen poised to write more notes.

"But that," the Change Agent pronounced, standing, "is for another time. For now, build relationships with the employees you already have—and between them. Remember—no one knows your business better than you!"

As the Change Agent left, closing the door behind him, Joan looked down at the list in front of her.

She had a lot of work to do.

CHAPTER 5

Joan worked with Carol to schedule time that would allow for everyone to be together for their first team day. Joan was anxious about not scheduling customers and having to pay everyone but hoped that this would pay off in the long run. If she could keep great stylists and avoid having to replace staff every six months, it would be well worth it.

Now, she just needed to make that happen.

She had announced the team day at the beginning of shifts the week before and explained to people its purpose. 'To let us get to know each other. To let us craft a mission statement that will take us to the next level.' Joan made it clear—she hoped—that she valued each and every one of her current stylists. She wanted to do everything in her power to make sure that they were happy here, as Ramone apparently hadn't been.

As she announced her vision to her team, the mixed reactions mirrored her own mixed feelings. Some of her stylists looked excited at the idea of creating something meaningful and having the chance to improve their styling game; others seemed nervous about what changes this might bring, and whether they would be asked to sacrifice some of their independence to this new team culture.

Joan remembered her own anxiety at making the first of her changes and reassured herself by remembering how well they had turned out. When she followed the Change Agent's advice, her salon was a happier, more supportive place to work.

She also remembered the Change Agent's words about employers "hiring people like them."

She hoped that her stylists would appreciate what she had planned as much as she did.

#

On Team Day, Joan closed the salon for the morning to allow her employees to spend some quality time with her and with each other. It felt strange to have everyone at the salon at the same time — stranger still not to have any customers during broad daylight.

But Joan began to see the benefits, even within the first hour. Linda started to open up a little, joking and laughing with her teammates. Theresa relaxed and seemed more at ease.

Joan laid out her vision of her company's culture for all to see. This would not simply be *a* hair salon: This would be the best salon in the country.

She passed out written copies of her vision description to everyone and tried not to appear anxious as she heard the "oohs," "aahs," and "hmms" in reaction.

To Joan's surprise, it was Theresa who raised her hand first.

"This sounds great and all," Theresa said, "but *how* exactly are we going to do it?"

Looking at Theresa's frown, Joan understood. Theresa was worried about her weekends.

"I'm glad you asked that question, Theresa," Joan said. "Because we're going to work on figuring that out today. Together. Everybody, I brought some pens and paper…"

In the hour to come, Joan began to read off the notes. Ideas were sorted into piles; ideas were fired back and forth over the table and discussed. A couple of heated debates broke out, but no one seemed the worse for it.

The Change Agent was right: Joan's team was *much* more engaged in the process since they were now part of it.

At the end of an hour, only one piece of paper was left, and it was in Joan's hands. It read:

Our mission is to…

- Help our clients become their best selves by offering stellar, industry-leading style, cosmetic, and relaxation services.

- Follow the path of continuous improvement by setting goals of learning new tools and techniques in our profession.

- Support our team members in achieving the personal and professional goals that are set.

- Commit to care for ourselves and each other just as we would our clients.

"We guarantee that our clients will walk out of our doors looking and feeling great! And, we know that to transform others, we must be our best possible selves."

As Joan read this final product aloud, Jacquelyn looked delighted, Linda looked cautiously optimistic, and Theresa looked suspicious.

"Now," Joan explained, "these statements make up our Mission. We will all work together to make these things a reality. But we need some SMART goals that need to happen *before* we can start realizing these. These goals should be:

Specific - An exact action that we can take and complete.

Measurable - There should be a way we can tell when it's done.

Achievable - Something we can do right now.

Results-oriented - Making our mission statement a reality.

Time-limited - We need to give ourselves a deadline."

Joan pulled out another stack of blank paper and her secret weapon: a tray of cookies, to keep the team's spirit up. "Now — who's got ideas?"

After some lively debate, the team decided on SMART goals of:

- Creating a 'before and after' board where stylists could show off their work and acknowledge the transformation of their clients. To be facilitated by Carol in the next 30 days.

    o Establish a ballot box where employees and customers can vote for best transformation of the month.

    o Each month's winner to receive a $50 bonus, facilitated by Joan.

- Joan will set up an anonymous suggestion box as a place for any employee to communicate their suggestions, concerns, and complaints to Joan directly, instead of venting to customers or each other.

- In the next two months, the whole team will develop a new employee hiring process where the team will be actively involved in the selection process and will be responsible for helping to make the new employee a contributing part of their team.

- o This will be done in preparation for hiring Ramone's replacement.

Ramone's replacement. The empty shift in the salon's weekly roster was causing quite a bit of tension, but Joan didn't feel ready to tackle that yet. Her hiring practices to date had obviously been problematic—something needed to change, but she wasn't sure exactly what.

She needed to talk to the Change Agent again.

So as the day's evening customers began to arrive, and Joan announced an end to the team day, she was relieved to see him among the people waiting in the lobby.

She retreated toward her office with the day's notes and motioned for him to follow.

"So," the Change Agent asked, falling into step beside her, "how did your first team day go?"

Joan waved her sheaf of papers. "Very well, thank you!"

"Congratulations!" the Change Agent beamed. "But," he continued, "I get the sense that there is something you would like to talk to me about."

Joan led the Change Agent into her office and closed the door behind them. "Yes," she said nervously. "It's hiring time."

The Change Agent nodded. "And so it's an excellent time to create and understand your new hiring process."

Joan sat down behind her desk, pulling up fresh paper to take notes on. "How... how do I begin to do that?"

"You tell me. Now that you have a mission statement and a vision for your company's culture, what do you see as the first step in that process?"

"Well," Joan said, "first I'd make sure every new employee understood and agreed to the vision, culture and mission statement. I want them to know *exactly* what's expected of them before they sign up. I'd also need to determine if they fit the company culture... but how do I do that?"

"There are a few ways you could," the Change Agent said thoughtfully. "One is to tailor your interview questions to reflect the company culture. If you want employees who help and support other employees, perhaps you could ask them to tell you about a time they did that at a previous job."

Joan scribbled that down. "That's a really good idea!"

"Another helpful tactic might be to have them shadow someone doing the work they are applying for. Try doing this during a very busy time of the day. It's important that they see what the work will be like — that way, there should be no surprises.

"After that, if they are still interested, you might want to see if they actually have the skills that they report on a resume. Creating a skills test will show if they can actually do the work at the quality you'd expect.

"For other positions like administrative, sales and customer service, there are assessment tools that can help you determine if someone has the thinking and behavioral styles for them to be successful within your business. Using these tools enables you to remove some of the 'gut instinct' that comes into play when making a new hire.

"Only after all those steps would I suggest that you involve your team members in the interview process. You may want to provide some guidance to your team about questions to ask and things to look for. Seeing how the interviewee interacts with the members of your team can be a good predictor of how they will interact in the workplace on a daily basis.

"If you give the prospective employee the opportunity to meet with other team members alone during the interview process, they may feel freer to ask your team members questions — and share their true feelings about the job's responsibilities — than they would feel if they met only with you.

"The final step in the process will be to get collective feedback from all the team members involved. Being slow to hire and quick to fire—if needed—will save time and money and will earn you the respect of your team, because you value the culture and the team members that honor that culture. Taking all these things into consideration before making an offer will give you a broad base of information to make a solid selection for the new team member."

"That makes good sense!" Joan exclaimed.

"But," the Change Agent cautioned her, holding up his finger, "the process of making sure your employee is successful does not stop with the hiring decision. You should also have:

- An onboarding process, including a checklist of everything your employee needs to be trained on to become effective and independent. This can include culture policies, such as how to interact with customers, as well as practical things like how to properly maintain equipment and use the company's operational and software systems.

- A new team member mentoring program. This would be an experienced employee—preferably the employee who is best at the job responsibilities most similar to those you want the new employee to fill. The employee should have thirty-minute weekly mentorship meetings with the new employee for their first ninety days.

- Weekly checkpoint meetings. These are short meetings that you have with the supervisor, mentor and new employee to review the training program and their progress. Your role is to identify challenges and help remove any barriers to the new employee achieving success."

"That's all so smart," Joan exclaimed, smacking herself in the forehead. "Why have I never heard any of this before?"

"The truth is," the Change Agent said, "most small businesses don't have a written hiring process. Only after they realize that the cost of searching, interviewing, hiring and training a new person who is not successful is about one year's wage, does the owner realize how important a successful and thorough hiring system is.

"As a business grows, the only way to scale and grow consistently is to add employees. And that often takes a different set of skills from what it took to start the business in the first place."

Joan nodded her head in understanding.

"You already have a strong team of employees. Many of them probably have strengths or skills you have not even noticed. They may also have job duties that you don't realize they have.

"This next week, I'd suggest you give your team members an assignment. Have them write down everything they do for your business hourly, daily, weekly, monthly, quarterly, semi-annually, annually and those things they do that only need to be done once.

"This sounds like it would be an exhaustive list, but in my experience, these take only about thirty minutes to complete," the Change Agent continued.

"With this information, you will have the data to create your positional contracts, job descriptions, and training programs for each position. The value to your team and the business will be immeasurable!"

The Change Agent stood and bowed slightly. "When you get your lists, we will meet again, to review the lists and to discuss how we can make your vision a reality."

Joan nodded respectfully as the Change Agent opened her office door to admit the happy chatter of the salon. He closed it behind him as he left.

CHAPTER 6

Over the next week, Joan watched her employees' task lists come pouring in. She encouraged them to keep notepads at their stations, so that they could jot down any task they might otherwise forget as they did it.

As the lists came in, Joan put all the lists in their appropriate files... stylists, massage therapist and nail techs. There were multiple lists for each. In addition, she had a list from Carol for reception/customer service and another single list from Sandy in accounting.

For the jobs that had multiple lists, Joan asked Carol to find a one-hour block in everyone's schedule over the next few weeks so that all people doing the same job could be together. Their task would be to review all the lists, consolidate them into one master list of responsibilities, and gain consensus that the list was complete for their position. When done, the list would be returned to Joan for review and final approval.

While those meetings were being held, Joan went over Carol's and Sandy's lists to see if there was any duplication or anything missing. As a result of these lists, Joan found that Carol was working overtime just to get all the work completed, and Sandy had some additional time with her current workload.

With that information, Joan had a short meeting with both Carol and Sandy to have them work out a training plan and work schedule which would give Sandy some additional hours at the registration desk and Carol would not have to work overtime, so she could go spend more time with her family.

When the master lists were returned to Joan, she blocked out an hour in her schedule to review the results and begin crafting her new job descriptions and positional contracts. As she reviewed the lists, she was fascinated to see all the tasks her employees did — many of which she hadn't even thought of.

By now, Joan had come to recognize the Change Agent's gentle knock on her office door.

"Come in," she called brightly.

"Hello, Joan," the Change Agent said. "I see you've got your lists in order."

Joan nodded, and her eyes returned to scanning the pages before her. "I've just started reviewing the final master lists."

"And what," the Change Agent asked, sitting, "have you learned from the lists your team provided so far?"

"Well, Carol's been working too much, and Sandy hasn't had enough to do — so Sandy's taking on some of Carol's duties."

"Splendid," the Change Agent praised. "You've begun to learn one important step to having a strong and resilient business: cross-training."

Joan looked up at the Change Agent questioningly.

"With an active cross-training program," the Change Agent explained, "you train each team member to perform other team members' duties. That way, if someone is sick, or your business experiences an unexpected change in volume of clients, your team members can fill multiple roles, if needed.

"From the master lists, you can make some tools to help you give your business this flexibility:

- **Positional contracts** - Positional contracts allow you to set a comprehensive job description for each job in your organization that will detail the unique terms of employment with consistent success metrics for each position.

- **Training checklist for each position** - These lists will help with both training new employees and enable consistent cross-training of existing employees who want to learn a new skill and add value to themselves and the business.

- **Standard Operating Procedures** - This is a written description of your 'best practices,' and shows exactly how each task is performed. If a new and better way is found, you update the procedures, and everyone does it that way.

- **Waste reduction** - By reviewing standard operating procedures every six months, you can ensure your team is efficient and does not lose time to outdated or redundant procedures."

The Change Agent leaned forward. "Having these things in place will help to ensure that you get employees who really want these job duties, and that the work will be done well. These things will take time to create—but ask your team to help write and develop them. The fastest way to create internal systems is when you are training someone for a new role. New employees are always taking notes. Make it part of their responsibility to share their notes with the trainer. When the notes are complete, those notes become the internal system for that task!"

As her vision statement, mission statement, and job descriptions came together, Joan began to imagine the start of her hiring process with eagerness instead of dread.

She pictured her employees talking to someone who was enthusiastic about the mission statement of her business, and eager to participate. She imagined finding someone who was excited to compete for 'best transformation.'

She imagined her staff training the new hire, with their mentor teaching everything from proper stocking and cleaning of the workstation to the tips and tricks of determining what would *truly* delight a customer. There was no way she could lose!

Joan was sure this would be a totally different experience from her previous hiring method. *That* had consisted of little more than a look at the candidate's work history and an interview to probe for any glaring problems. Then she'd put them in place, and hope they knew what they were doing.

Yes — Joan was sure those days were gone!

#

Joan's staff seemed just as excited when she shared their new hiring process with them. And she could see why! It had become clear to her, as she thought out the logistics, that better team members would mean easier lives for everyone.

After a week of interviews, a new stylist — named Michelle — proved to be the perfect fit. Michelle was fresh out of cosmetology school, like Linda. She loved the company's mission statement, and her eyes lit up when she saw the transformation board.

Joan thought that everything was going well — she watched fondly as her staff members trained Michelle in every aspect of being a stylist at her salon. But about a week into Michelle's training, discord erupted.

"*I* don't have time to train Michelle on the booking system," Theresa was saying hotly when Joan walked into the breakroom. "I'm fully booked today! I won't have a moment of downtime!"

"Well, so am I," protested Jacqueline. "And besides, I spent an hour with her yesterday, showing her the products in the back room. And by the way, *who* trained her in cleaning the workstation? She did mine yesterday, and she left hair everywhere!"

It was at this point that the ladies noticed Joan, who was standing with her eyebrows raised and her arms crossed. "Is there a problem?" she asked quietly.

Theresa and Jacqueline both looked a little embarrassed.

"It's just—" Jacqueline started, "we made lists of all the things Michelle needs to be trained on, but no one seems to have time to do it. Plus, some of the items on the list have been checked off, but we're not sure who did them. And Linda's supposed to be showing Michelle how to lock up some night this week, but she hasn't gotten back to me about which night..."

Joan pursed her lips. She'd spent a lot of time with the Change Agent; it was time for her to try to solve this problem on her own.

She remembered what the Change Agent had said about creating a 'clarity of expectations.' That was not something she'd done so far, because she'd thought she didn't need to. She'd thought her newly motivated team would work it out together.

Apparently, she was wrong.

Joan sighed, wishing she'd known better than to ignore a piece of the Change Agent's advice. She reached for Michelle's training checklist, which was hanging on the breakroom wall.

"Okay," she said to Theresa and Jacquelyn. "For each training task where you *know* who completed it, can you write that person's name by the check?"

The two complied. Joan was not surprised to see that Jacquelyn had done most of Michelle's training, while the other stylists' names were scattered randomly throughout. Joan started to go down the list, creating a rotation between the remaining stylists.

"Theresa," Joan said, "I'm going to need you to handle training Michelle on the computer systems. Stay late if you need to. It's just this once. And I heard you say that Linda isn't getting back to you about showing Michelle how to close up?"

Theresa nodded irritably. "I've asked her three times. She keeps saying she needs to check her schedule."

"Okay, then," Joan sighed. "I'll talk to Linda—" She was interrupted by a tap on her shoulder.

She jumped. So did Jacquelyn and Theresa.

"Where did you *come from?*" Theresa asked the Change Agent, who stood behind Joan, smiling politely.

"The same place I always do," the Change Agent said dismissively, before giving Joan a meaningful look.

"I have an—appointment with him—" Joan explained, half dragging the Change Agent out of the breakroom and back toward her office.

"Communication problems?" the Change Agent asked.

"Apparently!" Joan was still flabbergasted, and somewhat amused, by his sudden appearance.

"I think," he said politely, "it is time we had a talk about communication."

Joan sat down heavily at her desk. "How hard can communication be?" she asked. "I mean, I'm in the room with my employees. I talk to them. I tell them to ask me if they have any questions or concerns. After that the ball's in their court... isn't it?"

The Change Agent took up his usual seat, across from her desk. "Not quite," he said, with one of his finger wags. "Again, you are the boss; you are in charge of delegating and making sure that things run smoothly. In this case, if what you've done to communicate your thoughts and ideas didn't give you the results you wanted, then you need to look in the mirror and not blame others.

"After all," he reminded her, "your own behavior is the one thing you *can* control."

The Change Agent continued, "You could certainly argue, from a professional perspective, that everyone is responsible for their own communication. But that argument doesn't help your team work better. It only gives you someone to blame."

Joan crossed her arms.

"One option," the Change Agent said, "is to begin having MOMs."

Joan's eyebrows went up.

"MOM," the Change Agent explained, "stands for:

Morning

Opportunity

Meeting.

"A MOM is a fifteen- to thirty-minute meeting your staff has *each and every morning*, before your customers arrive.

"Morning Opportunity Meetings can include:

- An open review of the schedule - Any employee can speak up if they're aware of any changes, special needs, or opportunities for the day.

- An inventory of needs - Do any employees feel as though they, or their clients for the day, may benefit from special assistance? Are they aware of any shortfalls? If so, how will these be covered? This allows your team to plan together for optimal performance unique to the demands of each day.

- An inventory of opportunities - Are there any opportunities to grow your business today? Any clients who have been especially fruitful in purchases or referrals? Any open spots in the schedule that could be used to devote to a business growth task?

- A task checklist - For tasks that need to be performed each day, determine and verify exactly who will perform them and when."

"That sounds like a lot to do before we even start to see customers," Joan said worriedly.

"Fear not!" the Change Agent said lightly. "You may wish to create a clipboard with a piece of paper on it for each of those four components. Once your team is in the habit, your morning meeting will fly by—except, of course, on days that pose unique challenges, or opportunities for growth. And those are the opportunities you may miss if you do not adopt this practice!"

"Okay," Joan agreed, "Morning Opportunity Meetings might have made things a lot less hectic around here over the last few months. But what do I do about employees who *won't* cooperate—like Theresa and Linda?"

"That," the Change Agent said, "may be a product of their communication styles."

Joan pulled what she had begun to call her 'Change Agent notepad' into the center of her desk.

"Communication styles," the Change Agent continued, "are an important topic for business leaders to understand. This is another skill that no one teaches you in school—but can make the difference between an amazing, highly functional team and a frustrated, dysfunctional team.

"But it can be challenging when team members do not recognize the communication styles of other team members—or customers. Some people may be perceived as direct, rude or pushy, while others may seem as simply disengaged, or 'not team players.'"

Joan sat back thinking about this concept.

"I like to talk about four different types of communication styles and how they may relate to your employees," the Change Agent began. "As you may have guessed—I have an acronym! I use GOLF:

Golden Retriever - A reliable worker who looks for ways to help others and communicates honestly. Golden Retrievers—like your Jacquelyn—are wonderful in day-to-day operations, but they may not be inclined to take risks, and are more likely to try to make everybody happy than to point out problems when they see them.

Golden Retrievers are steady and consistent. They like to build relationships, and don't like conflict. They may not like to change very much.

Otter - Otters are social little creatures — have you ever seen the videos of them holding hands? Otters like to talk about emotions and relationships. They are willing to exchange ideas and can be great contributors of new views. The downside is that Otters may get frustrated and even rebellious if they feel ignored.

If I had to guess, I'd say your Theresa is a frustrated Otter. Communicating with her about emotional impact or strengthening relationships may be a way for you to reach her and help her understand her importance to this business.

Lion - Lions are the kings and queens of the jungle. They are no-nonsense types who strive for results and want to be the best. They are very often business owners because of their drive for success, but may not be the best team leaders because they may be impatient when things don't move forward the way they think it should.

Joan, you are a Lion.

Fox - Foxes are perfectionists. They take pride in the quality of their work, have great attention to detail and always make an informed decision. The downside is, they may be so determined to produce perfection that they work slowly, or hesitate to try anything new, and may hesitate to speak up when they are having trouble.

I suspect that your Linda is a Fox.

"We are all a combination of these four types," the Change Agent continued, "but usually we are more of one or two types than the others.

"When we understand how we like to communicate, and how others like to communicate, we can adjust our approach and style to be more effective. With a little training and time, we can educate your team on the different styles, so they can learn about themselves, their teammates, and their customers. When that happens, in my experience, communication within a business improves tremendously!

"Now," the Change Agent said, "based on that analysis, what are some actions you could take to help your employees understand and harness GOLF so they can understand themselves and get better communication results?"

"Well," Joan said cautiously, "I could listen to Theresa, and see what ideas she might have. And I could make a point of appreciating Linda's work so that she feels more confident in speaking up. But it sounds exhausting to constantly be managing employee relationships in this way."

"Exactly," the Change Agent said, satisfied. "That is why you're going to teach your team what I just taught you."

Joan looked down at her notepad. Recording the Change Agent's words had become second nature to her by now.

"I'll do that," she said. "Thank you."

CHAPTER 7

At first, Joan's employees weren't sure what to think about her new ideas.

The Morning Opportunity Meetings meant that the employees would have to arrive earlier than they had been—but Jacquelyn and Linda looked relieved at the prospect of having a place to strategize and plan their day.

Jacquelyn looked thoughtful as Joan explained GOLF and encouraged her employees to identify their primary communication style and share it with the others. Theresa looked suspicious; only Linda perked up.

But after a few weeks, Joan could see that *something* was working. Linda seemed happier and was speaking up more. Theresa had begun, grudgingly, to contribute more—Joan even caught her staying after hours once to clean her chair.

Joan was making headway on her goals—and she hadn't lost any employees since the Change Agent came into the picture!

She was enjoying a margarita on her front porch one night, and feeling good about her progress, when the Change Agent came hiking up her front lawn.

"Hi," she said. Though she was happy to see him, she was also a bit uneasy. Was she doing something else wrong that she hadn't realized yet?

"It's a beautiful evening, isn't it?" the Change Agent said amicably.

"It is," Joan agreed, sitting up. "Can I get you a drink?"

The Change Agent shook his head politely. "I've sworn off the stuff, thank you. But you enjoy yours."

Joan leaned back and watched the fireflies dance over her front yard. "So," she asked finally, "we've been at this a while. How am I doing?"

The Change Agent smiled. "That's an excellent question. How do you think you're doing?"

Joan frowned. "I see some good changes in the way things are working, but I don't know how to measure the progress."

"Every organization that wishes to grow and improve," the Change Agent said, "must have a way to determine how well it is doing its job. One way to do this for employees would be performance reviews. I recommend that you have these meetings every three months—for both your employees *and* leaders. In this way, the leaders—and the whole company—can grow and improve, just as its individual employees do."

Joan laughed. "One thing I liked about renting a chair from Sarah was that I didn't have to worry about performance reviews. I was my own boss."

"Yes," the Change Agent agreed. "But you were not trying to run a business—you were just self-employed. If you wish to grow your business, you must do so by hiring employees. And you must constantly be on the lookout for ways you can help them grow and do their jobs better!"

"Alright then," Joan relented. "Performance reviews it is. But what does that even look like?"

"An excellent question!" the Change Agent exclaimed. "I recommend starting with what is most important: your vision and culture.

"To create your evaluation sheets, take your vision and each of your culture points and put them on a page with a scale from one to ten. For each dimension, one is for non-existent while ten is for 'perfect.'

"A few days in advance of your review meeting, give each employee a copy and ask them to evaluate their level of performance on that scale. They are to have that completed by the time of your meeting. While they are making their list, you also make one based on your thoughts on where you feel they are on each scale.

"When you have your meeting, go over each scale and each of you share the rankings. If they think they are a seven and you rate them a six, there is general consensus. But, if they think they are an eight and you think they're a four — now you have something to talk about."

"Ask your employee to explain their self-rankings. Come to agreement on a fair number from both perspectives."

"When you've reviewed all your performance dimensions, pick two or three of the most important areas to improve and discuss things that the employee can *start, change* or *stop* to increase their scores by one or two levels.

"Write those improvement methods down on the review form and get your employee to agree that they will work on changing those things before the next review.

"Always make sure you remember to ask: 'What can I do to help you make those changes?' You never know what obstacles you had not considered may be standing in your employees' ways. Write down any changes you could make — without sacrificing other aspects of your business — on the form as well. And make sure you both get a copy!"

Joan chewed her lip, thinking about this. "But," she said, "if I was an employee, I'd be afraid to tell my boss if I thought they needed to improve. How do I know my employees won't just tell me what I want to hear?"

"That," the Change Agent pronounced, "is another excellent question. Remember your vision and mission statement? Didn't that include a focus on continuous improvement and open and honest communication? You see, a truly high-performing organization must cultivate a culture of transparency and honest feedback.

"Organizations that want to grow *must* have leaders who are genuinely open to honest feedback from employees. These are the leaders who get the most out of their employees' skills and observations. Leaders who are not interested in the opinions of their employees, on the other hand, will wonder why they are always so frustrated!"

"So how do I make my employees feel comfortable giving me honest feedback?"

"The simplest way," the Change Agent said sincerely, "is to be honestly interested in their opinions.

"If you are defensive and only want to hear feedback that agrees with your opinions, your employees will pick up on that, and will not be honest with you no matter what you do.

"If, however, you approach these meetings with a genuine sense of curiosity about what you could do better — and *willingness to change the way you do things* — you will notice very interesting fruits begin to emerge."

Joan looked out over her yard thoughtfully. That sounded difficult—but it made sense, and nothing worthwhile was ever really easy.

"There is one last thing I recommend," the Change Agent continued, leaning back in his chair.

"Oh?"

"You might try an incentive system, to motivate your employees to meet their goals and the goals of the business. What sorts of bonuses, recognition, or other perks could you offer employees who meet, say, four out of five of their quarterly review goals? What sorts of bonuses or recognition can you offer your entire team when your organization, as a whole, meets a growth or improvement goal?"

"Those are some big questions," Joan said thoughtfully. "But I'll bet I can think of answers."

"That's the spirit," the Change Agent said, smiling proudly. "The more you value your employees and listen to their honest feedback, the more your salon will be able to grow."

The Change Agent stood and stretched. As Joan watched, he pulled a black velvet bag from the pocket of his suit. He handed it to her.

Fascinated, Joan opened the bag, half-expecting to find some fancy piece of jewelry. Instead, she found a pewter and wood handmade pen unlike any she'd seen before.

"I think," he said, "that you have everything you need for your review meetings. But in case you find that you don't—just write down any question you might have with that pen. I will come to your assistance."

"I—thank you," Joan said.

She glanced up with a smile, but the Change Agent was already gone.

CHAPTER 8

Just like Joan, most of her employees were less than excited by the idea of performance reviews. Jacquelyn was fine with it; Linda and Michelle actually seemed interested.

But Theresa continued to quietly fume at any of Joan's requests, and Joan was starting to get seriously concerned about her. She had been hoping that Theresa's attitude would change as she instituted the Change Agent's suggestions, but sometimes this stylist just didn't seem to want to work here.

Joan didn't want to have to hire a new stylist to replace Theresa—though she planned to hire a new one *anyway*, since the business was growing.

But she didn't want to keep someone on her team who didn't want to be there, either.

Joan tried to ask herself: What would the Change Agent do?

Her employees—including Theresa, warmed up significantly when Joan announced her new incentive plan: Employees meeting four out of their five quarterly review metrics for success would receive a $500 bonus! It was a lot of money—but the costs would be covered by the increased productivity and, if it motivated her employees to do excellent work, it would be worth it!

Jacquelyn's performance review flew by without a hitch. As the Change Agent had predicted when he called her a Golden Retriever, Jacquelyn was largely on the same page as Joan about her own performance, was satisfied with Joan's support and communication and had no real suggestions for improvement.

Michelle identified a few areas for improvement — most of them related to her being new.

Linda's performance review was quiet, but perfect — just as the Change Agent had predicted in designating her a Fox.

And Theresa's performance review was interesting.

Joan started by rating Theresa as lacking in the 'supporting other employees' area. She explained that while Theresa's customers seemed happy with her work, the documentation from the scheduling system suggested that Theresa was avoiding working difficult and busy hours. And Joan mentioned that she had seen Theresa arguing with other employees in the breakroom — often over being asked to do her fair share of the team's work.

Theresa sat across the table from Joan and fidgeted. "I mean," she said, "I didn't become a stylist so I could work for somebody else."

Joan had to say she wasn't surprised. She remembered well how much she had enjoyed making her own hours and being solely responsible for her own clients.

"Then, Theresa," Joan asked, "why are you working here?"

And to her shock, Theresa began to cry.

Joan tried to think of what the Change Agent would do. *Always do what's best for business*, the Change Agent would say. *But never be cruel.*

"If you're so unhappy here..." Joan tried, "I mean, I don't think you should stay somewhere that makes you unhappy."

Theresa sniffled. Remembering the box of tissues by the door, Joan went and grabbed them.

"Thanks," Theresa managed, wiping her eyes. "I'm sorry, it's just—I didn't expect being a stylist to be so hard. I feel like I work so much, and people are still always asking me for more. I want to spend time with my friends and family on weekends, and I can't do that if I'm working."

Joan had to consider her next words carefully. She didn't know what was going on in Theresa's life—but she also had more than just her business to think about. Theresa's behavior was affecting her other employees negatively, and it was her job to protect them—not to favor Theresa.

"Theresa," Joan said honestly, "I want to keep you here. But it does seem like our team mission just isn't a good fit for what you want to do. Have you thought about being an independent contractor?"

Theresa looked down at the table for a long moment. "I'm not sure I could make it that way," she said honestly.

"Well," Joan said, "you have a choice. You can stay here—and support your colleagues the way they support you. But I can't have you pushing the hard shifts off on other people anymore. That's not fair to them. If I see you switch another weekend or evening shift—I'm going to have to let you go."

Joan was surprised how freeing it felt to say that. She had lived in fear of losing staff and having to hire someone new for so long—but now she felt like she was doing what was best for everyone, and she could see a clear path to hiring and keeping new employees.

But the meeting wasn't over yet. It was time for Theresa's review of Joan and the company.

Joan held her breath as Theresa pushed her company evaluation across the table toward her. To Joan's surprise, Theresa had rated the company well on most metrics, including 'customer satisfaction' and 'team support.' But Theresa had written a few suggestions for Joan to consider:

- Offer weekend and weekday shift options, so that employees work predictable days each week.

- Offer evening and morning shift options, so that employees work predictable times each day.

Joan looked at Theresa's suggestions critically. She had once refused to make set shifts like that, because she felt everyone should have to share the burden of the 'undesirable' hours. But she remembered what the Change Agent had said about being genuinely curious about her workers' opinions.

"Who do you think," she asked Theresa, "would want to work mostly weekends, or mostly evenings?"

"Plenty of people who are in school, or who have spouses who work night shifts," Theresa responded. "I used to work with a woman whose husband worked late shifts at a factory; she loved starting her work day in the afternoon and getting done late in the evening, so she could have her 'evening' after he got home from work.

"*I'm* not one of those people," Theresa clarified hastily. "But if you offered shifts *designed* for people in those situations, you could expand your business hours *and* it might give everyone more flexibility."

Joan thought about this.

"I have a friend who is in cosmetology school," Theresa ventured, "and she can't work during business hours on weekdays because of her classes. But she wants to get more hands-on experience and make some money while she finishes school." Theresa eyed Joan with an unspoken question.

Joan nodded as she considered Theresa's words. She normally only looked at stylists who already had their cosmetology degrees, but someone who wanted to work *while* in school sounded like she had quite a work ethic. And having a weekend-only shift person *would* make life easier for the other stylists, if she was a good fit for the business...

"Can you give me your friend's name?" Joan asked.

As Theresa left her review, Joan felt oddly relieved. Now she finally knew what was bothering Theresa — and maybe she *would* be able to expand her business hours, and give her whole staff more flexibility, if she took Theresa's advice.

Still, the process of giving performance reviews was emotionally draining. Joan was happy to go home and nap when the day was done!

#

The next day, Joan decided to treat herself. She left for work early and got a table at her favorite brunch place.

She was waiting for her omelet—and looking over yesterday's notes—when the Change Agent appeared beside her table.

"Is this seat taken?" he asked, placing a hand on the chair across from Joan.

"Please," she gestured.

The Change Agent eased himself into the chair, looking about the restaurant curiously. "What do you recommend?" he asked. "I've never been here before."

It was hard for Joan to imagine *anything* the Change Agent didn't know. But she recommended the pancakes.

"So," the Change Agent asked, "how did it go? How are you feeling about your business now?"

"I'm feeling... good!" Joan replied, surprising herself with her own enthusiasm. "There are bumps in the road... but there always will be, won't there?"

"Yes," the Change Agent agreed. "If life were always predictable, it wouldn't be much fun."

Joan told the Change Agent about her meeting with Theresa. To her surprise, he smiled broadly.

"You handled that very well, Joan! Sometimes, giving the employee the option, or even encouraging them, to 'deselect themselves' if you see the job is not a good fit is the best thing for both of you. Many employees spend their lives in jobs that make them unhappy because they are afraid to let their boss down or look for another job."

Joan nodded thoughtfully. "I never thought about it that way before."

"However, it also sounds like Theresa had a great idea. Sharing all hours equally is a good idea if your employees' lives are all the same—but if you can find employees who *prefer* different shifts, you can expand your business and offer your employees unique flexibility."

Joan nodded, smiling.

"So," the Change Agent began, as the waiter brought Joan's omelet and his huge plate of pancakes, "it sounds like everything is going quite well for you, actually. Are you ready to keep improving your team?"

Joan put her fork down. "There's more to do?" she asked incredulously.

"As long as you want to grow your business," the Change Agent responded, "there will *always* be more to do. You've made great progress and, at least for now, I don't think you'll need my help anymore! But I wanted to give you a few more suggestions to strengthen your team—and your mission—as you enter your next phase of growth."

Joan waited, a little anxious at the thought of not having the Change Agent to call on anymore.

"Now that you know how to use your vision and culture, your new hiring process, and the team-building communication ideas to help your business be the best that it can be, there are some ways you can make things even better:

- **Weekly cross-training** - Schedule 30 minutes each week for each team member to learn something new.

- Whether that means learning how other employees' essential tasks are done, shadowing another employee who does something particularly well, or doing some hands-on learning from a local school or internet tutorial, over time this half-hour per week will ensure that your clients have stellar experiences — even if a team member calls in sick — and your team's skills won't stop growing just because they're not in school anymore.

- **Make sure your clients know about your total commitment to serve them** - If you have not already, update your brochures, website, and other client-facing materials to make sure they know of your commitment to help them transform into the people they want to be and to keep your stylists up to date on the latest trends and techniques.

- **Always keep your door open to suggestions from your employees** - Very often, the same things that would make their lives easier would also cut your costs and make your team more productive!"

Listening to the Change Agent talk, Joan began to get excited again.

Taking time for skill-building would mean cutting a few client appointment slots each week — but she could see how it could rapidly result in a better experience for the clients she did have, and allow her salon to provide the latest styles, techniques, and unique services. And if she hired more employees — especially if she hired some who preferred evenings or weekends — she could offer appointment slots at new times, which she was certain she could fill very quickly!

As the Change Agent finished his pancakes, Joan found that she had tears in her eyes. This man who had come, seemingly from nowhere, had helped her transform her business in ways she had not thought possible.

As he stood to leave, she stood too, and clasped his hands. "How can I ever thank you for your help?" she asked.

The Change Agent bowed his head politely. "You can pay it forward. Someday, you will meet a business owner in need of guidance. Now, you'll be able to help them."

They walked together to Joan's car in companionable silence. Though he was still an almost total stranger, Joan was going to miss this man's visits. But—she was sure he had important work to do elsewhere. Perhaps another business owner to help.

By the time she pulled out of the parking lot, he was gone.

CHAPTER 9

It had been over a year since meeting the Change Agent, and Joan had booked a Caribbean cruise.

She could afford the two weeks away—her business was thriving, and without her constant oversight. She'd promoted Jacquelyn to the position of manager, and with the help of Theresa's suggestion, the salon was now open fifteen hours per day, seven days per week.

She had more customers and revenue than ever before without having to expand her facilities, and all her veteran team members showed fierce loyalty in helping new employees learn the ropes and ensuring that all shifts were covered.

The night before she was due to leave, Joan booked herself to work the salon's evening shift and close it up for the night. She wanted time to admire what she had done.

There wasn't much to do—her employees had gotten into the habit of cleaning up after themselves and making sure their stations were well-stocked at the end of their shifts. Joan made doubly sure that the schedule for the next week was solid—

including backup scheduling, in case one of her stylists had an emergency.

Then she took a deep breath. Jacquelyn could handle this. *She* could handle this. This is what freedom was all about.

On her way out through the front door, she stopped and flipped on the lights above the salon's Transformation Wall of Fame.

There, a dozen before-and-after pictures showed off how her business had transformed her clients' lives. Tired-looking middle-aged moms became smiling, pop star divas; shy girls became supermodels. Men, young and old, became dapper and suave. Wallflowers became bold and colorful.

Joan sighed happily, thinking about what each picture represented. With the Change Agent's help, she had made time for her stylists to learn the latest techniques and offer their clients looks that the competition couldn't.

Their mission statement had helped them focus on the client experience of transforming into who they wanted to be — not just on technical expertise or following the latest fashion trends. Her Yelp reviews had skyrocketed, and she'd been interviewed by a couple of local newspapers since the word of her salon began to spread.

A year ago, she would not have believed any of this was possible. She'd been struggling just to keep her head above water with miserable employees and some unhappy customers.

As Joan turned out the light and locked the door behind her, she resolved to do as the Change Agent had asked. Someday, she'd pay it forward.

JACK AND THE ELUSIVE RETIREMENT

CHAPTER 1

"Thank you so much, Dr. Williams!"

The patient's mom smiled at him gratefully. At her side, her six-year-old son held her hand while looking up at Dr. Jack Williams almost suspiciously. It *hadn't* hurt like his classmates had said it would, and his small patient seemed to be wondering if this was some sort of trick.

"David, what do you say?"

"Thank you," the little boy mumbled, embarrassed at being prompted.

Still, he clutched his sugar-free candy the dentist had given him and followed his mom out into the waiting room. As his mom stopped at the check-out desk, the little boy looked around, wide-eyed, at the decorations. In one corner, cuddly teddy bears, well-loved rag dolls, and sparkly unicorns huddled on a couch near a window. On the other end, fish swam in an enormous tank. The boy seemed to be considering that maybe the dentist wasn't such a bad place after all.

Dr. Jack Williams chuckled. One thing didn't change with time: His young patients had always been skeptical. But they often grew to enjoy coming back.

Any day when he made patients happy was a good day. But as he finished up his patient notes for the day, Jack was bothered by the thought of how much *had* changed — and how much was sure to change in the future.

When he started this practice thirty-five years ago — that time seemed like a different world. For one thing, people drank less soda and ate less sugar: He saw *that* difference every time he looked in a patient's mouth. People needed far more dental care than ever, it seemed. The increase in sugar consumption made ensuring his patients' quality of life more challenging, and more vital, than ever.

But things had been different in other ways, too. A patient-dentist relationship, back in the day, had been just that. Not a patient-insurer-dentist-relationship.

Back then, many patients had not needed insurance to pay for their dental costs. He had graduated as a newly minted dentist with no student debt, so he had been able to take a modest salary coming out of school, and the dentist he'd apprenticed under had been able to charge his patients lower rates.

Now, Jack was starting to think about retiring, just as his mentor had. But he had no associate dentist to sell his practice to — and finding one was proving difficult.

Everything seemed so much more complicated than it used to be. He had bought this business from its senior dentist—Dr. Michaels—after they worked together for four years. Jack had been looking for a little over a year for a new dentist to apprentice with him in the same way, and eventually buy his business—but they all told him the same things.

For one thing, all the newly graduated dentists now had huge amounts of student debt. Some told him they owed hundreds of thousands of dollars for their undergraduate plus dental school. They just couldn't afford to take the salary he was willing to offer, let alone buy the business from him in the next few years.

To pay the wages they were asking and compete with big chain dental practices, he would have had to charge his patients more, and cut back on offering them procedures that weren't covered by their insurance.

The insurance companies were partially to blame for that. They had trained people to rely on dental and health insurance to determine the

quality of their health care. Very few people were willing to pay for dental care except through insurance. Now, a great deal of his staff's time was spent educating patients about the things insurance did and did not cover.

The insurers were constantly changing the procedures they would cover—many did not cover procedures that Jack knew would benefit his patients. This left him with the choice of either not providing those services, or having the patients pay out-of-pocket.

For years, Jack's practice had grown its annual revenue at a double-digit rate. But now, that rate seemed unsustainable. To maintain that growth, he'd have to bring in about twenty new patients per month. He wasn't even sure he had the staffing to handle that many appointments!

Today, Jack smiled at his front office team as they left for the day. Most of these people had worked for him for years, and he knew their families. He wondered what the future would hold— who would manage his practice and be their boss in five or ten years, when he retired?

Once, his daughters had sat in those chairs. They'd worked at his practice just long enough to realize that they didn't want it to be their career. Now, Claire was in graduate school and Olivia was in the Navy. Without another dentist to take over, how was he going to retire?

His wife, Lynn, was eager for that day to come. She wanted to travel the world while she and Jack were still in good health. They'd tried to take a few trips so far, but without another dentist at the practice, things went downhill fast in Jack's absence. It was important to him that his patients kept receiving the treatment they'd come to expect—but he knew he couldn't keep working forever.

What was he going to do?

The thought of simply closing the business when the time came had crossed his mind. He had enough in his retirement savings for him and Lynn to live comfortably—just barely. But what would his patients and employees do then?

Jack had poured most of his life into this business, and dozens of people had come to depend on it. There must be a better way—a way he could benefit from all the years he'd invested so his employees could continue to have jobs, and his patients could continue to have a dentist they trust.

There had to be a better way. Jack just had to find it.

But how?

CHAPTER 2

Lynn still made Jack coffee in the morning. She was now retired from her part-time role as a dental assistant, and spent her days doing paintings that hung in local coffee shops and art galleries. Jack was glad she'd found something she enjoyed doing — but he wished he could spend more time with her as they got older.

He took his coffee — and a kiss from Lynn — and headed out to his car. Even though it was Saturday. He now spent six days a week at the office: five serving patients, and another day going over accounting paperwork, wading through insurance claims, and trying to find ways to add value to his patients' experiences without the insurance companies being involved.

Since it wasn't an appointment day, Jack was surprised to find someone waiting for him when he pulled into his practice's parking lot.

The tall, slender man wore an impeccably tailored suit. He was pacing back and forth on the office patio, appearing deep in thought. He didn't look lost — he looked like he was waiting for someone.

"Can I help you?" Jack asked warily, walking up to the door with his keys in hand. Sometimes drug company representatives came to visit uninvited. But visiting on a day when no one was supposed to be at the practice would be new.

"Ah, yes! Dr. Jack Williams?" the man queried, extending a long, graceful hand to shake.

Something about the stranger's manner was so friendly, Jack couldn't *not* shake it. The man's grip was firm.

"And you are?"

"I," the stranger said with a flourish, "am known as the Change Agent. I help business owners in distress. And I understand that you, Dr. Williams, have been having some difficulty in arranging your retirement?"

Jack looked around the parking lot suspiciously. He felt like the little boy, David, leaving his office yesterday.

"Who told you that?"

"I have my ways of detecting owners in distress, Dr. Williams. I understand your concern—confidentiality is *paramount* when preparing for a business sale. But I assure you, my methods are quite unique. And quite secure."

This fellow who talked like a movie character was oddly charming, and seemed harmless. Jack decided to let him follow him into the office as he unlocked the door.

"So, Mr. Change Agent. *How* exactly do you help business owners?"

"Why, with my insight and experience, of course! You see, I've built and sold quite a few businesses in my time. I've learned some very effective principals, practices, tools and techniques along the way. Now, I share them with others."

Jack eyed the Change Agent sidelong. The man didn't look like he could have been older than forty. Thirty seemed closer.

"Uh huh. And I suppose you're retired now."

"In a sense. Now, I need only do what I love!"

"So what's the cost?"

"Pardon?"

"The cost. Of your services. What do you charge?"

"Oh! I don't, Dr. Williams. That's the entire point of being *retired*, you see. The sales of my businesses have allowed me to function quite well without concern for payment."

Jack had to admit, he was suspicious, but impressed.

He let the Change Agent follow him as he wound through the darkened waiting room, down the halls with the exam rooms branching off of them. Finally, they came to his office, buried in the back of the building — and under stacks of papers.

The Change Agent peered around curiously. "Am I correct, Dr. Williams, that you would very much like to be rid of the business?"

"I think so," Jack confessed, "but I don't want to close it."

"You're eager to exit your business as quickly as possible, then?"

"Well... as quickly as possible, *provided* my employees keep their jobs. And their salaries. And my patients keep their dentist. *And* I can fund the trips I've been promising Lynn..."

"That all sounds quite achievable."

Jack looked up. "Excuse me?"

"Yes. What you've described is not difficult. *Challenging,* yes. But not difficult."

Jack plunked himself down in his chair and gestured for the Change Agent to take a seat for himself. "Please... explain."

"Well, Dr. Williams," the Change Agent said, dusting off the long-vacant seat, "it may surprise you to know just how many business owners share your concern. When the time comes that they no longer wish to run their business — or to work at all — most business owners are not sure how to proceed. In fact, there is a great deal of confusion about how a business owner should expect to retire:

- 14% of business owners plan to fully fund their retirement with their business.

- 19% of business owners plan to draw an income from their business after they've retired.

- 59% of business owners think they will achieve most of their retirement income by saving their current earnings.

- 40% of business owners don't save at all."

Jack sat back, shocked by that information. He couldn't imagine *not* saving for retirement. So at least he had a leg up there.

"When you are preparing to exit your business — that is, to sell it or pass it off to other management," the Change Agent continued, "there are a few steps that must be followed:

1. Maintain confidentiality. Employees and customers alike might start looking for a way out if they learn that your business will be changing management. Poorly planned business sales often don't go well for existing customers or employees. If your best staff leave, your business can lose quite a bit of value. So confidentiality is paramount!

2. Grow your business. Some business owners lose interest in growth when they begin planning to exit, but this is exactly the time to be encouraging growth. The more profit your business generates, the more a prospective buyer will be willing to pay you for it.

3. Know what your ideal buyer wants. This can sometimes be the trickiest part. Who is likely to want to buy a business like yours? Who is likely to continue providing great service to your patients? Why do they want to buy the business? What is their motivation?

4. Build your Exit Team. You should have a team of professionals that you can rely on for advice and counsel to help you make sure you get the most out of selling your business. We will talk in more depth about this later.

5. Know the value of your business. Members of your Exit Team can help you identify a price range for the business.

6. Manage your risk. We'll talk more about this later.

7. Write your exit plan. Your Exit Team will help you with this.

8. Review the plan regularly, to ensure you are taking all the necessary steps to make this plan a reality!"

Jack rubbed his temples. "That all sounds complicated," he said, "and expensive."

"It's not nearly as expensive," the Change Agent pointed out, "as continuing on as you have been. Not nearly as expensive as simply closing your business, instead of selling it."

"That's true," Jack admitted.

"So, Dr. Williams," the Change Agent said, "would you like my assistance in putting together the plan for you to exit your business?"

"I—yes. If you're willing."

The Change Agent beamed. "I most certainly am! In that case, the next step in this process is simple. Simply imagine—in great detail—what you want your life to look like after you sell your business. You can't make a thing real if you don't know what it is! So, imagine what life will be like when you don't have the business to be responsible for, and then, determine your needs—in terms of time, money, and other assets.

"Once you have your dream mapped out, we will begin making it a reality."

CHAPTER 3

That night, Jack bought a bottle of Lynn's favorite wine and took it home. He wanted to get Lynn's thoughts about what their life would look like if he was able to sell the business and retire. They'd talked around the subject at different times in the past, but, because it didn't seem possible, they'd never gone into detail. It would be an enlightening and exciting conversation, he was sure of that.

In the next few weeks, Jack spent a lot of time daydreaming about the variety of options he and Lynn had discussed. He had daydreamed about retirement plenty—about traveling the world with Lynn, standing on the decks of cruise ships and sitting in the backs of carts, trucks, and even on elephants as they saw the exotic parts of Africa and Asia.

He'd envisioned the sights and smells. Lynn had even begun painting some of them. She had a passion for savanna and jungle landscapes, and a gift for catching the character of wild animals. But for now, she was mostly limited to using pictures she saw on the internet as inspiration.

Now was the time for Jack to start writing down some details on what their life would look like in retirement:

- Working 0 hours per week

- $5,000 monthly income for 30 years = $1.8 million in the bank

- Inheritance for kids? Life insurance policies, $1 million x 2

- Travel 2-3 times per year to a variety of places around the world

As the Change Agent had suggested, he kept his plans confidential. There would be plenty of time for sharing later.

But he knew, in theory, that it *should* be possible. If owners of other types of businesses could sell their businesses for millions, why couldn't he?

Knowing he would see the Change Agent again, Jack also kept a list of questions in his desk drawer. The Change Agent had given him a lot to think about, and he tried to think of what questions he should focus on in their next discussion:

- How much is my business worth?

- Who would be interested in buying my business? How will I make that happen?

- Who will run the business if I'm not here?

- Can I really sell my business for the amount of cash I need for my retirement?

- How do I keep growing my company's value so that I can sell it for more?

As Jack worked on his list, he continued to see patients. His patients ranged from very young to very old — from people with good dental health who wanted cosmetic work, to people who needed a lot of dental help. He found himself looking ahead and worrying. Even if he wanted to keep working instead of retiring, he was getting older. Who would look after his patients when he was gone?

Jack was ecstatic one day to see a new face in the waiting room. The Change Agent bowed politely when he saw Jack come into view behind the receptionist's desk.

"Mr.... Agent!" Jack exclaimed, coming out to greet him.

"Dr. Williams," his receptionist began, "I don't see him in the appointment calendar..."

"He's not a patient. He's a... different kind of appointment."

Dr. Williams led the Change Agent back toward his office. Somehow, the man had managed to pick a time when Jack had a rare opening in his schedule. He was really going to have to ask the Change Agent about his methods someday.

"Welcome back." Jack gestured for the Change Agent to take his seat across from Jack's desk. He reached into his drawer and took out his list of questions.

"Yes, many good questions," the Change Agent murmured, looking over the list. "But," he asked, "before we can answer these questions, we need to know what you want your life to look like. Do you have that list with you?"

Jack produced the list of what he wanted his retirement to look like.

"Very good," the Change Agent murmured. "Very good."

"So," Jack asked finally, "where do we start?"

"An excellent question," the Change Agent replied, straightening from where he'd bent over the papers. "The key in all cases is to *start now*. It will take some time to accomplish all the things that will need to be done—those who plan ahead and take time to evaluate their options always get the best deals.

"I told you last time we met that we would discuss your Exit Team later. That time is now. Your Exit Team will be a group of professionals that can provide advice and counsel on their area of expertise.

"Your Exit Team should include the following:

Your Business Team

- Business attorney - An attorney will be needed to create buy-sell agreements, key employee agreements, and customer contracts.

- Business accountant - Your accountant will help you create strong financial reports for all parts of your business. They will also be one of the best resources to provide options on the value of the business.

- Business banker - Your banker can help you explore options for funding the purchase of the business and resources needed for your growth strategies.

- Business insurance broker - Your insurance broker can reduce risk and help provide protection against losses in the event of catastrophe.

- A coach/consultant - Someone needs to be the quarterback for this team. It will be their job to ensure that everyone is doing their part to make your plan happen, so that the business owner can maintain focus on growing the business. A coach/consultant who has helped other business owners with the same process can help you be aware of the options, ask the right questions, and avoid common pitfalls.

- Technology expert - Technology is changing fast, and businesses that don't keep up can be at risk for security breaches and falling behind the competition in efficiency. Technology experts can also help you value your company's technological assets, including the hardware and software your business uses.

- Key employee - Though it's a good idea to keep your plans to sell under wraps, if there is a key employee that is an integral part of the business, it may make sense to have them involved on the Exit Team.

Your Personal Team

- Personal attorney - This attorney specializing in retirement and estate law can assist you with putting together your estate, will, and any trust you may wish to create. If something happens to you, these documents will ensure your wishes will be carried out.

- Financial planner - Your financial advisor can help you create a solid and realistic financial picture for your post-business life. They are trained to ask the right questions and be able to put a plan together to achieve your goals.

- Insurance agent - This person will help you evaluate different types of personal insurance like life, health, disability, and long-term care. All should be considered to be part of your plan. Remember — insurance is the primary tool to manage the risk of what could happen.

- Tax advisor - Taxes are inevitable. When you sell your business, you need someone you can trust and that understands your situation and the impact that action will have on your personal tax liability.

"You will likely need all of your team at some time during the process, but only a few of your team will be needed for your regular meetings.

"Selecting the right people is an important task, and the business owner needs to be comfortable with the team's decisions. For that reason, I recommend that you:

- Start with people you know and trust to fill the roles.

- Ask those people to refer others to you that they know or trust, or that they have heard good things about.

- Ask your network to make recommendations.

"After all this, if you still need to find a professional to be on your Exit Team, you can explore your industry associations or professional organizations.

"Before your first meeting, it is important that you prepare some basic things to ensure the confidentiality and sustainability of the process:

1. A non-disclosure document that all team members will read ahead of time and sign at the first meeting. Your business attorney can help with this.

2. A rough idea of the past few years' performance of the business, including a balance sheet, income statements and details on current debt. Your business accountant should be able to help with this.

3. An idea of what your monthly expenses will be after you complete the Exit Plan from your business. Your personal financial advisor should be able to help with this.

"Once you have chosen the members of your Exit Team, you will want to make sure they know, and understand, your goals. It will also be important for them to know the other members of your Exit Team, so they know who they can speak with about your plans.

"Have them suggest aspects of the plan where they have areas of expertise or resources that they could share. Your team members may be able to find opportunities you would not even have thought of—but they can only do that if they have a clear vision of exactly what you want.

"Once your team knows and understands your goals and you have had a few meetings, you will work with them to build the plan to make your dream a reality. Your experts will be able to provide options that you'd likely never have considered if you were working on your own.

"Your plan should include provisions to manage your risk—this means making plans to account for all the things that might go wrong. The plan should protect yourself, your family, and your business in the event that something unexpected happens personally or professionally.

"One of the most essential things your Exit Team will do for you is to help you value your business. Hopefully, giving you an idea of how much your business is *realistically worth to a buyer.*

"In reality, your business is only worth what someone is willing to pay for it. Knowing this number can ensure that you don't sell your business for far less than it is worth, not realizing its true value to a buyer.

"And of course," the Change Agent smiled, "the only true constant in life is change! Your Exit Team should meet regularly to review your plan and determine if milestones are being met, and if changes are needed in the plan."

Jack winced. "That all sounds REALLY complicated," he groaned.

"That," the Change Agent said, "is why you will break it up into small steps. Let's make a to-do list:

1. Identify a list of potential Exit Team candidates and conduct interviews with them—three hours per week over the next month.

2. Ask your network for referrals of any of the Exit Team positions that don't get filled.

3. Work with the Exit Team to create effective and efficient ways to share information. If these people are going to invest their time to help, you don't want to waste any opportunity, or their time.

4. Once selected, bring the Exit Team together and share your retirement goals—your vision for the future of your business *and* your family.

5. This should happen in about two months. Pick a date far enough out that will give you the best chance of not having scheduling conflicts. These are busy people, and their calendars fill up fast!

"At your first meeting, you'll want to:

- Create a list of quarterly goals to move the project forward for the next four quarters.

- Schedule regular meetings with key members and quarterly meetings with everyone to evaluate progress."

Jack looked at the Change Agent's list. It still looked like a lot to do, but now that he knew exactly *what* to do, it seemed achievable.

"Your first task," the Change Agent reported, "is to assemble your Exit Team. Find the candidates who you trust and feel will be best at looking after your personal concerns and sensibilities. Set a date for the first team meeting in about three months!"

It felt odd to be given an assignment—Jack tried to remember how many years it had been since he'd been in school.

But this was an assignment he'd gladly accept, if it allowed him to get paid for the years he'd spent building his business!

CHAPTER 4

Over the coming weeks, Jack carved out time to make phone calls. He talked with his accountant, and she was very happy to help. He did speak with his banker and found that they had some resources at the bank that would be of great benefit to the project.

He asked his friends, family and business associates for recommendations for good attorneys, insurance agents, and other experts. He spoke to several on the phone, and a couple in person who had offices near his house.

Thinking of it like an interview process helped. He wasn't there to get *their* approval for his retirement ideas, he reminded himself. They were there to gain *his* approval.

When he'd finally made his selection, Jack started thinking about how to get all of them in one place. Meeting at the dental practice during business hours sounded risky — surely his employees and customers would get nervous if they saw half a dozen lawyers and insurance agents filing in!

But he hit on a solution: He would have his team clear a block of time on his calendar for a Friday afternoon. Then, they would meet in the conference room at the country club. The club could provide the privacy they needed and a nice lunch. And, if they wanted, they could golf after the meeting.

As Jack greeted the members of his team as they filed into the conference room, the reality of what he was doing started to hit him. He'd long dreamed of retiring with Lynn, but in those fantasies, the business simply didn't exist, or it somehow went on without him just as it always had.

In his fantasies, he was simultaneously Dr. Williams, dental practice owner — and Jack, adventurous husband of Lynn. The idea of selling the business he'd spent thirty-five years building had never really been a possibility before. But, now, with everyone's help, Jack was cautiously optimistic.

Now that all of these well-dressed professionals who sold businesses and moved assets for a living were gathered in here to help him, he felt honored — but also a little scared.

He remembered the Change Agent's words. This was the way to make his dream a reality. This was his team. He had to keep thinking of them that way, as *his* team, not intimidating authorities on subjects he knew little about. He was in charge.

He tried to feel like it as he stood in front of the team. As the staff brought water, coffee, and iced tea and took everyone's lunch order, Jack prepared to make his speech.

"Thank you all for coming," Jack said, "this is a very important day for me, my wife Lynn, and my dental practice.

"As we all know, none of us are getting any younger. I've been running this practice for thirty-five years—and I don't think I have another thirty-five in me!" That got a few smiles.

"You've all agreed to be part of my Exit Team. The team has a single mission… to help me successfully exit my business. Part of that will be to find a new owner who can take over so the practice can keep running as it always has.

"This is very important to me—the new owner *must* keep the practice running with the same standards of excellence to patients and employees that I have established.

"Everyone in this room will have a role to play in developing and executing this plan. You all have an area of expertise, and I need your advice. You may know of people who might be interested in purchasing this business—so please keep your eyes and ears open.

"It is imperative that the things we talk about stay between the members of this team. If this information was to get out before the right time, it could be devastating to my business and my employees."

Jack nodded to Lisa, his business attorney, who sat near the head of the table, just to his left. "If everyone agrees, please sign one of these non-disclosure agreements and hand it back to Lisa."

Now, it was time for introductions to begin. "Lisa is a business attorney who specializes in business sales and employee contracts. This is Frank..."

He went around the table, introducing everyone to each other. Many handshakes and smiles and business cards were exchanged. The team members treated each other with professional courtesy.

Then came the moment of truth. It was time for Jack to pull out his list of personal and business goals he had written.

The business goals read:

- Continue serving patients with the same care and attention to preventative dental care that we currently provide.

- Continue current employees under identical employment agreements, including pay rate, benefits, and retirement packages, for at least five years.

- Continue double-digit business growth the practice has seen in recent years until the time the sale is complete.

The meeting lasted several hours as each member of the team contributed their thoughts about the next steps to take to make sure Jack had ironclad contracts and good prospective buyers. Jack took meticulous notes.

At the end of the meeting, he felt exhausted—but empowered. The future of his business was in his hands now, and he really felt like he could shape it into anything he wanted.

"Thank you for being part of my team. I will send out the notes from this meeting to all on Monday." Jack began to circle the table, handing out business cards with his private phone number to call if they had any questions.

"Get together again in about a month? I'll send the next meeting date with notes."

Everyone happily agreed.

CHAPTER 5

Over the next few months, leads for potential business buyers came pouring in from members of Jack's team. Jack had set up a special phone number to handle these calls, so they didn't come to the practice phone.

The prospective buyers ranged from businessmen who were known for acquiring small business empires to a local dental student who 'might think about it.'

Jack kept meticulous notes on all these candidates, but soon found himself overwhelmed. There were some who clearly had the money, but who he feared wouldn't care about his business, patients or employees; others had their hearts in the right places, but he couldn't imagine how they would raise the money needed to purchase the business.

He had taken his papers to a local coffee shop to get a change of perspective one day when a familiar figure walked in.

Jack felt his whole body relax as he waved to the Change Agent. Surely his mysterious mentor would know what to do!

The Change Agent ordered a cappuccino and made his way over to Jack's table. "Good afternoon," he greeted Jack cheerily, "how's it going?"

Jack looked up at him nervously. "Um, well. I felt like I had things under control—but when I look seriously for people to buy my business, it starts to feel pretty hopeless. Who has both the money and the heart for it?"

The Change Agent sat across from Jack and leaned forward sympathetically. Jack shoved his papers in the Change Agent's direction, glad to be rid of them.

The Change Agent leafed through Jack's notes, his eyebrows rising higher and higher as he did so. "Well. You *do* have an array of candidates here. I can see why you're concerned. But, maybe there is a way to make sense of these options—and zero in on the candidates that are right for you."

The Change Agent began, "There are a few categories of people who usually buy businesses when it comes time for the founder to retire:

- Key employees - Just like you purchased this practice from Dr. Michaels, there's no one better for the business—and no one who stands to gain more from purchasing it—than a long-time employee who knows the business's clients, vendors, and other employees.

- Family members - Family members who wish to keep assets in the family often purchase businesses owned by their parents, aunts, or uncles.

- This can be a comfortable way of handing down a legacy and keeping wealth within the family. Although, it doesn't necessarily ensure that the practice falls into hands that are skilled or experienced in business.

- Financial buyers - These are people like your businessmen here, who see the businesses they acquire as an investment. They may take a hands-off approach, letting your employees run the business as they please, so long as the business keeps growing and provides a good return on their investment.

- On the other hand, with financial buyers there is always a risk that they may make drastic changes to the way your business runs. To a financial buyer, your requirement to keep current employment agreements in place for five years could be a deal-breaker.

- Strategic buyers - Strategic buyers look at a business specifically because they're interested in the industry or business model. They might be looking for a way to get into dentistry, or to add new offerings to their existing business model.

- These buyers may care a great deal about the service you provide, and may even be knowledgeable about your industry."

Jack frowned. "My daughters don't want the business, and neither do any of my existing employees. I don't want a financial buyer who just sees my business as a set of numbers. But how do you find a strategic buyer? I have no idea who would want to buy my business and have the money for it!"

The Change Agent smiled. "Oh, yes, you do," he said.

Jack stared at him blankly.

"Think about it. Who would love to turn your patients into their patients, if they could?"

"Well, Dr. Li down the street, and Dr. Jones over in Northville. They are both really good dentists with great reputations."

"Precisely!" the Change Agent beamed. "Now, if they could buy your practice — keeping the staff employed and patients happy while providing new opportunities for their existing staff — do you imagine that they might be interested?"

Jack thought about this hard.

It made sense. Other business owners within his industry would already know how to run the different parts of a dental practice, from serving patient needs to marketing and working with suppliers. And since he'd be leaving most of his connections behind, it would be relatively little work for them to simply let most of his staff continue what they were doing.

"Yes…" Jack said. "That could work."

"Now," the Change Agent held up a cautionary finger, "the search for a buyer for your business should be looked at as a marathon, not a sprint. Just like when you were interviewing members of your Exit Team, form a list of potential buyers and weigh the pros and cons of each before approaching them.

"You know lots of dentists who run practices in your area. You know because you hear about them from your patients. Consider what you've heard about each one—which would you *most* like to have take over your practice? Rank them in order of your preferences.

"I suggest that you ask the members of your Exit Team if *they* know anyone who might be interested. Who knows! Maybe they know some dentists you don't."

Jack found himself feeling at ease once again.

But he wrote down a new note on the back of one of his papers. *Ask team – rank local competitors.*

CHAPTER 6

The following week, it was time for the next meeting of Jack's Exit Team. He had made a list of six dentists in the area who he *knew* wanted to grow their practice, and who he'd heard at least some good things about from patients.

As his Exit Team filed into the country club conference room for a second time, his business attorney looked over his list approvingly.

"That's very good," she said. "Now—how much do you want for the business?"

Around the room, eyebrows raised. Jack knew that he *could* give a number of what he'd like to get for the business, because he knew how much he'd need to fund his retirement travels with Lynn. But the Change Agent had warned him *not* to do that.

Instead, the Change Agent said, he should ask his team how to determine the true value of his business.

Jack looked up at the team around the table. "What I'd like for the business is not as important as what the current value is to the potential buyer. What I'd like you to do is tell me how much it might be worth. Truthfully, that's one of the reasons you're all here."

Jack's accountant was the first to speak up. "There are hundreds of ways to estimate the value of a business," the man said. "The value speaks to a few things—how much revenue it generates, how much profit will come from that revenue, the value of any hard assets, and how dependent the business is on the owner to generate profit.

"Some industries have standard formulas that can be used when selling. But one common formula uses your EBITDA times a coefficient multiplier."

Jack blinked. "EBITDA? That's a mouthful."

"EBITDA," his accountant explained, "stands for:

Earnings

Before

Interest

Taxes

Depreciation

Amortization.

"It is a basic accounting number that represents the amount of money your business brings in each year, before it interacts with any accounting adjustments.

"The multiplier is not as easy to explain. The range of the multipliers is between 0.5 and 8.0. The number is based on how well the business functions without the owner working in it. That represents the business's value—relative to the amount of work the new buyer would have to put into it—after you've left.

"If you were able to sit on a beach and collect a check each month without doing anything to help manage the business, the multiplier would be close to an 8. On the other hand, if you did everything in the business, your multiplier would be 0.5.

"If the practice depends on your production, you will need to figure in how much you contribute to its annual earnings. If that number is significant, the multiplier will be lower than you might expect."

"Oh," Jack looked crestfallen. "Well, I generate—gosh. With the junior dentist and my two hygienists, I'm about forty percent of the production of the practice. From what I hear you telling me, this is a problem?"

"Not," his exit consultant piped up, "if you hire a new head dentist who will stay with the practice and do most of your work when you leave it.

"This sort of thing is exactly why it's a good idea to start planning for sale five to seven years *before* you want to actually retire. Thinking about these kinds of things in advance lets you make changes to your business structure that will allow it to be worth much more money."

Jack gave a task to his Exit Team. "I'd like you all to put your heads together and come to me with two price ranges. The first range will be based on the way things are structured right now."

"For that," the accountant said, "everyone will need your current financial reports, a list of equipment and current valuations, and the EBITDA numbers for each of the past three years."

Jack nodded. "You have all that information — please share it with them. The second price range will be based on hiring a head dentist that will take over my production work and maintain the double-digit growth rate we've had in recent years. We have the EBITDA numbers in my financial reports, but the one number that needs to be determined is the multiplier.

"Make sure your estimates also include the value of the hard assets, like the building we work out of — we do own that, we're not renting it — and the depreciated value of the practice's equipment.

"There is a great deal of expensive equipment, and the values as of the end of last year are included in my year-end reports."

Jack looked at his Exit Team members, who were nodding to themselves and taking notes.

"Okay, does everyone understand what I'm asking for?" Jack re-capped to make sure they all understood.

Everyone nodded.

"Good. Then when can I expect the numbers?"

His team gathered about the conference table and pulled out phones, calculators and notepads. It took about a minute, and then Lisa responded and said, "We can get you those numbers in the next thirty days. Probably sooner, but we can commit to thirty days."

Jack nodded, satisfied. "Thirty days it is. Thank you."

Jack continued "So... to raise the value of my business, I need to hire a new head dentist to take over many of my work hours. But this doesn't need to be someone who's interested in buying the practice from me — it can just be someone who wants to work as an employee for a salary."

His exit coach nodded. "Correct."

"Alright, then," Jack said, pushing his chair back. "I'll ask Lynn to help me work up a job description for an associate dentist to take over the team. If possible, we'll start interviewing potential new dentists this month."

Jack stood.

"Thank you all for your input and help with this. It sounds like everyone has their assignments. I'll see you all in about a month!"

CHAPTER 7

Jack started advertising for a lead dentist and also started working with a recruiter to help speed the process of finding a qualified candidate — preferably someone with five to ten years of experience under their belt, and able to start soon.

Within two weeks, Jack had some possible candidates to speak with, and he planned to set up one-on-one interviews after normal practice hours.

In those face-to-face conversations, he explained what he was looking for and found that it was easier to offer a high starting salary to a new dentist when he thought of it as a big investment in the value of his business.

The interviews were interesting. One candidate had been laid off by a neighboring practice that was experiencing financial difficulty. Another had quit, saying his last boss was impossible to work for. A third didn't have the experience Jack had desired — but had applied anyway, promising she could learn to do anything Jack could in a matter of months.

After that last interview, Jack felt torn. He watched the young woman go. She'd had stellar grades in dental school and an impressive track record, including a publication in a peer-reviewed journal. He felt she'd work harder than any junior dentist he'd worked with in a long time. But could he really leave his business in the hands of two relative rookies when it was undergoing a change of management?

Jack was delighted — and somehow not surprised — to see a new visitor rise to his feet as the candidate closed the door behind her. The Change Agent headed for Jack, just as though he'd had an appointment.

"Welcome!" Jack exclaimed, throwing open the candidates' resume folders for the Change Agent to see. "I just can't decide who to pick," he explained. "The first candidate sounded experienced — but this one's a real go-getter. What will my business need more of when I'm gone?"

The Change Agent looked ponderously, not at the resume, but at Jack.

"Well," he asked, "how soon do you plan to leave?"

Jack had been afraid the Change Agent would ask that. He'd thought about it himself — and he just wasn't sure. Part of him wanted to complete this process and go traveling with Lynn as soon as possible. Another part was reluctant to take his hands off the steering wheel of the business that he had spent the last thirty-five years building. Given this indecision, finding out the ranges for the value of his business, Jack thought, should help.

"I... let's say a few years?" Jack suggested.

The Change Agent pursed his lips. "That seems reasonable. But let's see what your team of experts has to say about it, first."

As though at the Change Agent's command, Jack's phone rang. His accountant's name showed up on the caller ID.

"Hi—Jack? I've got your numbers."

His accountant went on to explain:

The first number was the way things were right now, with Jack doing most of the dental production.

The team estimated the value at an EBITDA multiplier of .75 – 1.0.

The second number they were asking for was the multiplier that would apply if he hired a head dentist that would do Jack's production work.

Under those conditions, their estimate was an EBITDA multiplier of 2.5-3.0.

Jack listened and nodded. But as he nodded, he realized something: Because of the additional payroll expense, the EBITDA would be initially less. It would be some time before hiring a lead dentist could significantly increase the value of his business.

Jack sat in his chair, taking notes of the phone conversation.

Hearing the information shared by his accountant, Jack realized that the idea of staying in the practice for more than two years *really* didn't appeal to him. The time he could spend with Lynn was precious. He would take a lower price for the business if he was able to be gone two years from now.

He filed that away to put on his list of 'goals and visions.'

"Okay," Jack said, taking a deep breath and hanging up the phone. "So, I'll get back to these candidates after I speak with my team next week."

The Change Agent nodded. "And?"

Jack just looked at him. "And?"

"There's something else," the Change Agent said gently, "that you could be doing to protect yourself and your business."

Jack sat back in his chair and waited.

"Risk management," the Change Agent began, "is the way you protect your business, your employees, and your family against the possibility of something unexpected happening."

Jack frowned. "Unexpected? Like what?"

"Well," the Change Agent said delicately, "you're putting a lot of plans in place, but what would happen if your health takes a turn, or heaven forbid, something worse happens? If you can't work, or can't make decisions, what will happen to your business and your family?"

Jack thought about that. He had life insurance that would go to support Lynn and the girls—quite a large policy, too. But he had nothing in place to protect the business, and even his hefty life insurance payout was starting to seem like small potatoes next to the potential value of his business.

And what would happen to his employees, if something happened to him? How would he be able to ensure his patients were cared for?

He tried to remember if he'd ever designated who would take over the business in that event, or if he had any idea what would happen to it.

In his mind's eye, he saw a terrible scenario playing out. With no legal successor to the business, who would carry out the work and make the important business decisions? Would anyone on his staff even be legally allowed to handle his accounts if he passed away?

"That's why you suggested I get a financial planner, insurance broker and attorney as part of the Exit Team," Jack guessed, "isn't it?"

The Change Agent nodded graciously. "That is one of the reasons, yes. If you can determine a way for your business to continue if you are not able to work anymore, your employees, patients, and family alike will be better off. For that, you will need a will — among other things."

Jack nodded thoughtfully. "That's a good thought. Thanks."

"So, speaking to your attorney about risk management," the Change Agent reiterated, "is your first order of business. Your second should be hiring this new associate dentist. Once in place, they can help protect your practice if anything should happen to you. But just as important — can you guess what I'm going to say?"

Jack blinked and shook his head.

"It is important that you *continue growing your business* just as you were before. Slowing or stopping the growth rate will have a negative impact on the value of your business — the value of your business could drop by quite a bit."

Jack nodded sagely. "Continue to grow my business. Right. But…" he said hesitantly, "there aren't enough hours in a day to do all this!"

The Change Agent grinned. "That," he said, "is why you need a new dentist."

CHAPTER 8

In the coming weeks, Jack struggled to focus on his business and avoid giving any hints that he was planning to sell. Sometimes it was a challenge, with so many questions about increasing his business's value on his mind — but seeing the smiling faces of his patients and employees was always enough to get him in the moment.

His Exit Team plans *seemed* to be coming along well, but as time passed, Jack felt like he was hiding from something. The question of who would buy his business — and what they would do with it — still didn't feel resolved in his mind.

Would one of his competitors really want his practice, and be able to pay the price he was asking for it? Should he be talking to a bigger business with more cash — even if it meant they might change much of what he'd built? Or should he have been looking for an associate dentist who could give him *part* of the business's value instead of trying for a payout that still seemed, to him, impossibly big?

Jack was fretting over these questions — and trying not to show it as he finished up a young woman's dental exam — when Anna knocked politely on the door frame.

"Your—ah—friend, is here to see you. I put him in your office."

Jack knew exactly who she meant.

He sent the smiling woman on her way and consulted his calendar. His next appointment had called earlier to cancel, and he had no more patients scheduled for a couple of hours.

How had the Change Agent known? Regardless, Jack was glad to see him.

He entered his office to find the slender man snacking on a box of donuts. "Want some?" the Change Agent offered.

"I—yes, actually." Jack had to admit that comfort food sounded like just the thing for his sale-related anxiety.

The Change Agent watched him knowingly. "Having a tough time adjusting to the idea of selling?"

"I just don't know," Jack started, "who'd be willing to buy the practice."

"I understand your anxiety about finding a buyer," the Change Agent continued. "There are many options to choose from, and all have pros and cons. They also have different desires.

"By understanding the desires of your buyer, and being clear on what is important to you, you'll know when there is a good match.

"Let's revisit what we know to be true about your current situation. From what you've shared with me, you have no employees that have a desire to own the business, and your daughters are not interested. It doesn't sound like the family member or key employee option is for you."

The Change Agent continued, "As we discussed, financial buyers want to pay as little as possible for the business. But they will see it primarily as a financial investment. They don't really care about the past; they want to know what the business will be able to do in the future. These types of sales are like selling a house — the new owner gives you a check, and you give them the keys. Given your concerns over your employees and patients, it doesn't sound like this option will work for you, either.

"The third general category for business buyers is strategic buyers. The strategic buyer is buying the company because they want to enhance their existing operations."

Jack nodded thoughtfully. "So... I should be *able* to demonstrate that my practice does great without me, because of my employees and the systems we have in place?"

"Yes!" the Change Agent nodded. "When you can demonstrate how well your employees work together and that the business can work without you there — that's when a buyer will be willing to pay more money to acquire ownership of your business!

"Give it a few quarters with your current staff before you begin approaching prospective buyers. When you can prove that your business is doing something extraordinary — because of your employees, not because of you — then you will likely get a higher price for it."

Jack nodded thoughtfully.

The Change Agent reached into the box and grabbed another donut. "Helpful?" he asked.

"Very. Yes."

"Excellent!" The Change Agent stood, taking a huge bite out of his treat. "I'd better leave the rest of these with you — I can't seem to stop myself!"

Jack shook his head, chuckling, as the Change Agent let himself out.

#

As the days continued to pass, Jack still didn't feel at peace. He realized, slowly, that finding a buyer wasn't the only thing that had been bothering him. The smiling faces of his job applicants stayed with him, too.

He had really liked both the experienced dentist and the new graduate with such impressive accomplishments under her belt. She seemed like she would be full of new ideas for how to expand his practice, make more money, and increase efficiency. But the experienced candidate seemed like he'd be more of a leader and could keep the place running smoothly—a skill set that would be badly needed when Jack exited.

Jack thought about what the Change Agent would recommend.

In business, Jack had always assumed that less is more—that spending less money, when possible, was better. But he was hiring a new associate to increase the value of his company. The more value his company had—the more patients, and the more satisfied they were— the more attractive it would be to buyers, and the more money he would have for his and Lynn's retirement.

Thinking about what the Change Agent said about growth, Jack decided to take a gamble and hire *both* candidates. He recognized that this would be an investment in growth and the potential value of the practice.

If they were both as good as he thought they were, both would more than cover their costs with increased production. And, if he had the new dentists take over his patients, it would give him more time to work on his exit plan.

In addition, with the new dentists, the practice could expand hours, so they could see more patients than with the current schedule. The experienced dentist could become the team leader, and the new graduate might help him grow and expand the practice in ways he'd never even thought of in this rapidly changing world.

Jack was sitting at his desk, feeling pretty good about his decision and anticipating making the phone calls to offer both candidates the job.

Suddenly, there came a knock on his office door.

"Come in!" He had a feeling he knew who it was.

Sure enough, it was the Change Agent who opened the door and peered inside.

"So," he asked enthusiastically, taking his usual seat, "how is the retirement planning process going?"

Jack smiled, but also sighed a tired sigh. "There are a lot of things in the works, but I'm not sure I see the end of the tunnel, yet. I... I do have two things I'd like to share with you, and hear your opinion of."

First, Jack relayed the outcomes of the interviews. "They both seem really great, just in different ways. I think they might be perfect together. But paying costs for two new full-time dentists *is* a big investment..."

The Change Agent nodded wisely. "You're correct," he agreed. "This is an important decision. I cannot make it for you. Consider your desire to be out of the business in the near future and the need to continue to grow. Which of these options would get you there faster?"

That seemed clear, when the Change Agent put it that way.

"Certainly," the Change Agent continued, "you have to also consider your current team and the increased payroll. But, from what you shared, the two new producers will cover their costs and increase your business's profit margin significantly. That sounds like growth to me!"

Jack nodded, relieved that the Change Agent agreed with his decision. Maybe he was getting the hang of this cost/benefit analysis thing after all!

"The second thing I wanted to talk to you about," Jack hesitated, "was a chance meeting I had with Dr. Li. We were at a convention together last week, and we took time to have a cup of coffee together. We talked about some of the new technology that Dr. Li was using for his practice, which is primarily cosmetic dentistry and some specialized training that he and his staff have been taking to treat his patients.

"I took the opportunity to ask some questions about his practice, his patients, and some of the things that I had heard he was doing very well. When the conversation touched on my practice, I let him know that I had been considering the future and looking at a variety of different options. He asked if I had ever considered selling the practice.

"When he did, my heart skipped a beat. I was so excited, but I don't think it showed. And although he had expressed interest in learning more, I didn't know what to tell him or ask him.

"We finished coffee and agreed to connect in the next few weeks to have further discussion of the possibilities. But I don't know what to do now."

The Change Agent smiled a broad smile. "Don't worry. You did just fine. Just because he asked doesn't mean he's going to be the buyer, but it is a possibility. He sounds like one of many potential buyers you will have the opportunity to meet in the next couple of years.

"The most productive thing you can do when you find yourself talking to a potential buyer is determine what is important to them. Learn about their vision and what changes they see ahead of them.

"Ask Dr. Li about his patients and the services that he offers them; are there things he'd like to offer that he currently cannot — and why? Learn about his team and the strengths and weaknesses they have, if any. Treat this next meeting like an interview — you are interviewing *him* to see if he will give you what *you* truly desire, and if you can give him what he wants in return. Learn as much as you can.

"If he is interested in the possibility of buying your practice, he will be asking you similar questions. Be as honest as possible, but not specific with your answers. Your objective is to learn enough to determine if his practice and yours are a good fit for services and culture.

"There will be a time in your next conversation when you will both know whether you want to take things to the next level or walk away. If that manifests, acknowledge that, and suggest that before the next meeting you each sign a mutual non-disclosure agreement. Your business attorney will be able to draft one for you.

"That will provide some formality to your future discussions and be the trigger for each of you to share financial information.

"Remember — he may be interested in buying your business, but you need to know about the resources he has available to make the purchase.

"If that third meeting with Dr. Li happens, we can talk about the agenda and what you need to ask."

Jack was almost bouncing in his seat with the excitement. Could this really be happening?

The Change Agent smiled fondly but cautioned him not to get his expectations up too high. "Remember, this was a marathon, not a sprint, and you don't want to emotionally exhaust yourself early in the process.

"Reaching your exit planning goals," the Change Agent explained, smiling, "will take time. There's no need to rush! Enjoy the journey!"

The Change Agent stood, and Jack glanced at the clock by his desk. Just in time for his next appointment!

"Congratulations," the Change Agent said, "on making steady progress toward your retirement goals. There is much more yet ahead of you — but you have come far!"

Jack reflected that he really had. A few months ago, none of this had seemed possible. Now, it was forming into a reality!

#

To celebrate his progress with Dr. Li and his decision to hire the new associates, Jack decided to take Lynn out for a really nice dinner.

Lynn loved to dress up. He'd learned long ago that it wasn't that his wife loved makeup and clothes; it was that she loved to embody different characters. He knew she'd be as at home riding on the back of an elephant in a pith helmet as she was now, sitting across from him at a five-star restaurant and looking, as his daughters put it, like a "silver fox."

He was so lucky to have her — and he wanted to give it all to her.

He explained his hiring decision to Lynn, and she smiled. "I think that's a great idea," she said.

"Do you?"

"Of course. You've got to spend money to make money." She raised her wine glass.

As he watched Lynn shine under the soft lights of the restaurant, Jack realized that now was the time to tell her of his plans. He cleared his throat.

"Lynn," he said softly, "I have a big announcement to make."

She looked at him attentively.

"I'm planning—I mean, I think I've found a way, to sell my practice."

He waited for her reaction. Half-expecting, for some crazy reason, disapproval.

Lynn's eyes went wide. "Like—quit for good? Oh, Jack. How? When?"

He reached across the table to take her hand. "I don't know the answers to your questions, yet. I'm working with a team of people that are helping me to build its value. It will take a year or two, but I think I'll be able to sell it for—enough."

"Oh, *Jack*. After you sell it... can we travel?"

"That's why I'm doing it this way."

Lynn seemed stunned.

"Oh."

He squeezed her hand and looked directly into her eyes. "There is one thing. We can't tell *anyone about these plans. Even the girls.* I'm searching for a good buyer—someone who will take care of the staff and won't make drastic changes to the way things are done. So, this stays between you and me. Okay?"

Lynn nodded.

As Jack watched her, a new thought occurred to him. "Lynn, when I retire—when we don't *have* to live here anymore—where do you want to live? Really?"

Lynn got a faraway look. He wondered what continent she was traveling to.

"Honestly, Jack?"

"Of course, 'honestly!'"

"I'd love to keep the house our girls grew up in. Keep it as a nest to come back to. For all of us. I imagine someday we'll be too old to travel." The twinkle in her eye told him she expected that 'someday' would not come for a very long time.

"Since we talked about traveling a few times a year, I've been exploring options."

Jack nodded his head curiously.

"There are all kinds of websites now, I guess, where you can rent rooms or apartments or even houses all over the world. You can also book guided tours and experiences that are off the beaten path. We could live in a different country on each trip, Jack. Or maybe move a little less often than that. But it seems like there's no reason we couldn't visit *everywhere* that strikes our fancy — if we have the money."

Jack nodded thoughtfully. Five years ago, he'd have thought that sounded crazy — they'd lived their whole lives in one place, with him working one job. But now the Change Agent had shown him he really might be able to exit his business and travel with Lynn — and he'd heard the costs of living were lower overseas.

"I'd like to try that, Lynn," Jack agreed. Then he laughed. "I don't know how *long* I'd like to try it, but we can figure that out as we go along. Right?"

Lynn smiled. "Right. Once you're retired, you get to choose."

CHAPTER 9

Over the next year, getting ready to sell became Jack's new normal. He settled back in to seeing some patients and giving his new hires, Dr. Perez and Dr. Hobbes, the opportunity to drive the practice.

Jack knew completing the sale was going to take time, and he started planning to gradually reduce his involvement in the business. He and Lynn were able to take a few short vacations that gave the team the opportunity to work together without Jack being there.

In fact, Dr. Perez had developed a way to significantly reduce the time dealing with insurance issues by hiring an intern just to handle them. The intern quickly became an expert, and their time was much more affordable than dentist time. Dr. Perez also proposed a new ad campaign in underserved local areas as well as offering free exam days periodically to attract new patients who would not otherwise go to the dentist for fear of the cost.

Dr. Hobbes was well-liked by employees and patients alike. Over the past five years, he had built a strong following of patients that came to Jack's practice to see him. He was also experienced at finding the best solutions when new problems arose.

As these improvements were implemented by the team, Jack watched in disbelief as his practice's growth rate almost tripled to a projected 30%!

The members of his exit team were impressed, and in their ninth meeting, Jack mentioned his conversations with Dr. Li about purchasing the business.

"I've had a number of meetings with Dr. Li talking about what it would look like for him to buy my practice. He is a strategic buyer, and there seems to be a very good fit when we look at both businesses working together. He likes the location of my practice because there is enough room to bring both his practice and mine under one roof, and we have plenty of parking.

"We met three days ago," Jack recounted, "and both agreed that it was time for my Exit Team and his people to get together and work out the details. This is it!"

Jack looked to his coach, attorney, and accountant. "I would like you to work with Dr. Li's team to come up with details of a deal that is fair to all concerned. This needs to be a win-win, for Dr. Li, my employees, my patients and me."

Walking out of his Exit Team meeting, Jack held his head high. All the time he'd been pouring blood, sweat, and years into his business, he had actually been building wealth for his family! He was sure he'd never have realized how much—or gotten his time's true worth—without the Change Agent's help.

Jack was heading to his car when he met the Change Agent again. The peculiar, dapper man seemed to just materialize from the sunset shadows.

"Hello, Jack," said the Change Agent cheerfully. "I trust everything is going well?"

"Hello!" Jack enthused. "Yes, yes — my two new dentists are fitting in great, and Lynn and I are planning a two-week trip in the next few months. That will give us the opportunity to test the internal systems of the practice. If it goes well, I'm probably going down to part-time myself as my next move."

The Change Agent nodded approvingly. "Very good. It sounds like you're making progress on removing yourself from the business."

"Yes," Jack exclaimed. "When I thought about it, I really wanted to retire as soon as possible. I only wish I'd started planning to sell five years ago. I could have grown the business so much more, and so much faster! Before, I only ever really thought about how much work I could handle and increasing profits for myself. I never thought about growing the value of the practice to *sell* the company until you came along!"

The Change Agent nodded wisely, walking beside Jack as he headed to his car. "Yes, that is the way most people think. Most of us are taught that the way to get ahead in life is to be a worker —

not an *owner*. We think about how we can make money off of our labor. Not off of the *assets* we've created."

Jack shook his head. "I'm glad it's not just me."

"Far from it." The Change Agent allowed a slight pause to pass. "Any progress in your discussions with Dr. Li?"

Jack updated the Change Agent on the directions he had just given Lisa and the accountant, then shook his hand. "I can't thank you enough for all your help in making this happen," he said earnestly. "I'd never have gotten here without you."

The Change Agent raised his eyebrows. "Are you still sure you want to sell?"

"Yes. I think so, but the devil is in the details — that's why I have Lisa."

The Change Agent rubbed his hands together. "Then it is time," he announced, "for my final lesson." Out of nowhere, he produced a list, typed in old-style font. "This lesson is about your assets. There are several types of property values you need to consider when making a sale:

- Hard assets - These are any physical property that come with your business, including any office space and parking space you might own, and any physical equipment.

- Soft assets - These include people, skills, knowledge, intellectual capital, and any software or patents developed for your business.

- Goodwill - Goodwill is a type of soft asset that refers to the value of your reputation. Goodwill assets include logos, phone numbers, customer lists, trademarks, customer relationships, and any other value that the buyer receives from buying the reputation you have built for your company.

"I'm sure your Exit Team will understand these things and take them into account when determining a valuation.

"*You* know that your business has far more value than the monetary value of its hardware. Make sure that your *buyer* also understands the tremendous value of your patient relationships, your employees, and other assets that make your business far more profitable than it would be through hardware alone."

Jack looked at the list in his hand. Within the next few months, he resolved, he would sell his business. And he knew he would be leaving it in good hands.

The Change Agent reached into his suit jacket and pulled out a velvet bag. He offered it to Jack, who took it, frowning. He was surprised to open it and see an elegant pewter and wood pen. He'd heard of fancy pens being given as graduation gifts, but as retirement gifts?

"If you have need of me in the future," the Change Agent explained, "simply write down your question or concern on a piece of paper, using that pen. I will be there for you."

Jack looked down at the pen in his hand. It was hard to believe that this was — possibly — goodbye.

"I can't thank you enough," Jack said, "for all your help in making this happen. I'd never have gotten here without you."

Jack looked at the pen and felt the finality of it. Within the next few months, he resolved, he would sell his business.

And he knew he would be leaving it in good hands.

CHAPTER 10

Dr. Li was ready for business when he arrived at Jack's practice on a Friday afternoon. It had been two years since the Change Agent had come into Jack's life, and his business was, indeed, deeply changed.

Dr. Li had confided that he'd always seen Jack as one of his fiercest competitors — but, he said, he'd never expected to have the opportunity to acquire his business.

Dr. Li's acquisition team and Jack's Exit Team settled on a sale price that was fair. The EBITDA multiple that was agreed upon was 2.6. That number turned out to be a little more than what Dr. Li had been thinking, but he didn't say no. He said he'd have to think about it.

Jack's Exit Team told him he could have talked to multiple prospective buyers and started a bidding war. But Jack didn't want to sell his practice to just anyone. He wanted the buyer with the best reputation among his patients. So, he waited a week for Dr. Li to provide a definitive answer.

Dr. Li called and asked for a tour of the facility. Jack invited him on a free clinic day, to prove a point. The waiting room was packed with people from the less affluent parts of town, who wouldn't normally have seen a dentist regularly.

At the receptionist's desk, the insurance intern worked with patients to determine the lowest rates they could get them on the procedures they needed and presented options to work out payment plans.

Jack's regular patients came and went in the midst of it all: a local businesswoman who said she didn't trust anyone else with her family's dental health, a local realtor who said that having a brilliant smile was crucial to building trust with her clients.

Dr. Perez was on the job, delighted at getting the opportunity to treat new clinic patients, and Dr. Hobbes was effortlessly managing Jack's regulars.

Dr. Li was impressed with the practice, and with Jack's team.

"You know," he said on the way out, "at first, I thought you were asking far too much for this business. But I had no idea you'd grown so much. And you say you are only working—how many hours here?"

"Ten hours a week," Jack confirmed. "The practice pretty much runs itself, thanks to my team. Nothing would happen without them."

Dr. Li extended his hand. "I respect what you've built here," he said. "If the offer still stands, I'll take it."

Jack grinned. "It's a deal."

Shaking Dr. Li's hand felt unreal.

"Can we plan," the other dentist asked, "for a six-month transition?"

"I think we can make that work."

Jack felt a mix of sadness and elation as he walked away from the clinic that day. He'd spent over thirty-five years of his life making this practice the best it could be, caring tirelessly for patients and finding ways to save them money. He hadn't expected it to pay off this well financially — but then, he'd *never* thought about retirement.

It was sad to leave the practice — at some level he felt like he was giving up all he had built and earned.

But now was a time to open a new chapter in his life. He'd done his duty to his patients and employees — arguably more than done it. He'd spent his life using his skills to help people.

Now, Lynn was waiting for him.

AFTERWORD

Thank you for reading *Change Your Business, Change Your Life*. I hope you have enjoyed it—and more importantly, found it helpful for your business! I hope that every business owner can see a little bit of themselves in Mary, Mark, Joan, or Jack.

If you've come this far, you likely already are a business owner, or are considering becoming one. I do hope this book assists you on your journey—and I want to provide you with another resource to help you reach your business goals.

I am something of a Change Agent myself.

For over twenty-seven years, I have worked with small businesses or owned them myself. The stories contained within this book are representative of the things I've seen—including tools and tips that work across all industries.

A book is great, but there's no substitute for an experienced mentor. I want to make myself available to you for a free, thirty-minute conversation about your business and your goals.

I will tell you how to reach me in just a few moments, but first, there's an exercise you can do by yourself, at home.

This exercise can get you on the path to success, no matter where you are in your business journey:

1. Find a pen and pad of paper and sit somewhere quiet for 30 minutes.

2. Write down the things you read in the parables that you thought might work for you or your business—just the key words to help you understand your own thoughts about what's most important.

   These are your goals. These are the things you want to address, to develop in order to bring your business in line with your vision for your future.

3. Once your list is complete, or as complete as possible, prioritize the goal list.

   1. Put #1 next to the thing that has the potential to add the most value to your business or your life.

   2. Then find #2, then #3, and so on.

4. After you've prioritized the goal list, take a fresh sheet of paper and write your #1 prioritized goal across the top.

   1. Below the heading, write down all the things you'll need to do to make your goal part of your business or life.

   2. Then prioritize that list.

5. Then do the same thing on a separate sheet for #2 on your first list.

   1. Don't move on to the other goals until you complete both #1 and #2.

Find four hours a week to work on these things you've listed. Schedule the time in your calendar and get to work building a new habit.

This do-it-yourself exercise can help you get the most out of your time — and clarify what the most important things are that you might wish to ask for my advice on.

I can't magically materialize in your office or give everyone who reads this book a special pen. But I am willing to talk with you for thirty minutes about your situation and share some ideas on how you might address it. All at no cost to you.

I have been blessed to have wonderful mentors, friends, clients and strategic partners that understand the value of Paying It Forward and Giver's Gain. I am a true believer and am willing to help you in any way I can.

If you have the Desire to Grow and the Willingness to Change, let's see what we can do together.

You can reach me through my website, www.ABCBizCoach.com.

I hope to hear from you — and learn about your business — soon!

What things did I read about that will apply to my business?

Made in the USA
Lexington, KY
19 August 2018